T0058474

Traces of
Modernity

Traces of Modernity

Dan Smith

Winchester, UK
Washington, USA

First published by Zero Books, 2012
Zero Books is an imprint of John Hunt Publishing Ltd., Laurel House, Station Approach,
Alresford, Hants, SO24 9JH, UK
office1@o-books.net
www.o-books.com

For distributor details and how to order please visit the 'Ordering' section on our website.

Text copyright: Dan Smith 2010

ISBN: 978 1 84694 813 8

A CIP catalogue record for this book is available from the British Library.

Design: Stuart Davies

Printed in the UK by CPI Antony Rowe
Printed in the USA by Edwards Brothers Malloy

We operate a distinctive and ethical publishing philosophy in all
areas of our business, from our global network of authors to
production and worldwide distribution.

CONTENTS

Acknowledgements

This book has emerged from a long-standing set of interests which have been reshaped over a number of years. This period spans my studying as a part-time MA student in the late 1990s, the writing of my PhD, and the birth of my two children. I thank my wife Ann for her enduring patience and support, and my children, Hannah and Herb, for accepting that I have to spend so much time sitting in front of a computer.

A significant influence, for good or bad, has been my former tutor, and now colleague and friend, Neil Cummings. If any one individual is to blame, it is him. Neil's undergraduate seminars and lectures at Chelsea College of Art and Design in the first half of the 1990s resonated with my own unformed interests, and set in motion what was to follow. He also managed to teach and write in ways that were accessible, relevant and entertaining. I have since struggled to imitate him in these ways. Thanks are also due to Norman Bryson, who in the relatively short time he taught at the Slade School of Fine Art, was generous and never patronising. Over time, Donald Preziosi and Linda Nead offered some harsh but useful criticism on some of the ideas here that overlap with my PhD research.

I am in debt to the engaged students who have discussed and challenged the ideas presented in this book over the past decade or so, particularly in the courses on material culture I have taught at the Slade and Chelsea. Ideas are kept alive in these exchanges, and much is owed to them. I hope I have not plagiarised them. I am also grateful to Zer0 Books for providing an opportunity to put these strands together in one place, something that seemed for a long time to be at odds with the increasingly targeted strategies of many other publishers. I am genuinely excited by what Zer0 Books have been doing, which seems to be opening up new spaces for writers and audiences to trade ideas.

The ideas explored in Chapters 1, 2 and 3 were first put into a published form in the periodical *Things*. A special acknowledgement is due to *Things* editor Hildi Hawkins, from whom I learnt a great deal through her tactful suggestions. It was also Hildi's idea to write on the Pitt Rivers Museum, which enabled me to engage with something that had long been a source of fascination and appeal. Without the support and encouragement of Hildi, and the space provided by *Things*, this book would not have been written. Additionally, a differently weighted account of *The Time Machine* has appeared in *Exploring the Utopian Impulse: Essays on Utopian Thought and Practice* (Edited by Tom Moylan and Michael J. Griffin, Peter Lang Books 2007). The recent collection, *Cultural Memory: Reformations of the Past in the Present, and the Present in the Past*, (edited by Malcolm Miles and Vardan Azatyan, University of Plymouth Press 2010) included a piece on the Albert Memorial, which stands as a version between that presented here as the first chapter and my initial reflections on it, also published in *Things*. I would like to thank University of Plymouth Press for permission to reprint that material.

Preface

In the final version of *Berlin Childhood around 1900*, Walter Benjamin (2006) recalls how he was able to stage an adventure within the confines of his own room through the exploration of his wardrobe. He would delve inside among the nightshirts and undergarments, until he was able to find and remove pairs of socks, rolled up and turned inside out. Each of these became for him a small pocket, which contained a little present. Benjamin describes first grasping this present within, composed of a woollen mass, and then unveiling and unwrapping the present as it is pulled out from within the interior. Disconcertingly, as the present was revealed, the pocket would, of course, disappear. Yet rather than linger on this often repeated process as a confession of a psychically revealing compulsion, Benjamin recalls this memory to demonstrate its pedagogical impact, and the importance of this odd game in relation to his thinking in later life. This present is not like a toy wrapped in shiny paper, but rather is the tangible sense that inside the rolled up sock, is indeed, more sock. Within the interior space of the exterior is something that is indivisible from exterior. This is not just an infantile aporia, but is, according to Benjamin, the means by which he learnt about how to practice criticism:

> I could not repeat the experiment on this phenomena often enough. It taught me that form and content, veil and what is veiled, are the same. It led me to draw truth from works of literature as warily as the child's hand retrieved the sock from 'the pocket'. (Benjamin 2006, p.97)

There is on the one hand a specificity of interior and exterior that informs this book, in part on the level of indivisibility of form and content, but also the thematising and enacting of a dissolution of boundaries. However, there is a more pertinent instruction in Benjamin's memoir. This is the not to say that an object should act as an illustration of discourse, but that the pleasure one takes in an object can embody, perform and instruct acts of critical agency.

My own objects of illumination are vestiges of an event that played a large part in the shaping of the modern world. This book offers critical engagements with four objects from the nineteenth century: The ruins of the Crystal Palace in Sydenham and the dinosaurs that remain, the Albert Memorial in Kensington Gardens, Oxford's Pitt Rivers Museum and the short novel by H.G. Wells – *The Time Machine*. These provide very different forms of encounter, but are bound by the shadow of the Great Exhibition of 1851. This immense spectacle helped forge our understanding of display, surveillance and commodity. This legacy of what was a brief but dazzling event can be detected in the development of the modern museum and gallery as well as the shaping of spaces and structures of trade, commerce and political display, denying any possibility of conceptually separating these sites. Linked by a cumulative narrative that binds the mid nineteenth century to the early twenty first, these four objects are identified as formative traces of the past within the present. They provide models for critical thought and readings of the problematic conditions that they present as ideologically specific relics from a previous age. Each of the four chapters is an attempt to ask how to read the material presence of history. The selected objects are addressed as forms of material culture that can be brought to speech as reflections on criticism.

In *The Life of Forms in Art*, Henri Focillon argues that a quotidian normalisation of chronology has been habitually extended into historical organisations of time, as a necessary means of construction to secure the possibility of meaning. Stated intervals both classify objects and events and facilitate their interpretation. For Focillon, days, weeks and months offer the evidence of their own beginnings and endings, providing inalienable authenticity to reckonings of time:

> We are exceedingly reluctant to surrender the isochronal concept of time, for we confer upon any such equal measurements not only a metrical value that is beyond dispute, but also a kind of organic authority. These measurements presently become frames, and the frames then become bodies. We personify them. Nothing, for instance, could be more curious in this respect than our concept of the century. (Focillon 1992, p.138)

Focillon proposes that this model of time has the tendency of shaping centuries within the ages of a human life, parenthesized by birth and death. Time is organised according to a known architectural plan, allocated galleries and display cases as in a museum, and is moulded into discrete and efficient partitions. Focillon described the status of artworks as forms that rise proudly above forms of interpretation thrust upon them, establishing history as an immutable order. Focillon concedes that under such conditions a wilderness of criticism may spread up around an artwork. Flowers of interpretation conceal rather than adorn. In response, I would like to suggest the need for acts of criticism that attend to forms of material culture - those things that create the world - which can help to illuminate, reveal, and engage with forms that are profoundly generative. While the objects discussed in the book have demonstrated, performed, and perhaps enforced time as a configuration of modernity, the book itself is an attempt to de-partition the authoritative units of time in favour of a more disruptive temporality.

Chapter 1

The Gilded Man

As an undergraduate student at Chelsea College of Art and Design in the early 1990s, I often used to pass by what I considered to be the most interesting piece of public art in Britain. It stood at around 200 feet tall, towering over the surrounding trees of Kensington Gardens and seemed to exemplify a possibility for sculpture in the landscape. It was an ominous, challenging, melancholy presence. Incongruous, yet firmly rooted amongst the ornate greenery. It felt like this giant form embodied the end of minimalism, taking a category of artwork and realising the term's implications as a building type. Freed from the intentionality of art, the legacy of minimalism was instead manifested as an unconsciously driven visual and material sensibility for transforming London's past into a bold and dynamic future. I longed for a world that could be transformed in the image of this peculiar structure. What lurked inside was nothing more than an ostentatious, gaudy relic of Victoria's reign, consuming money and resources, an obese cocooned parasite.

For eight years the thing inside remained encased in a dense network of scaffolding. This mesh of tubes and planks was itself clad in tough protective layers of plastic. It was predominately opaque, with a suggested abstract form defined in dark green against the pale off-white. A central column on each side was transparent, revealing the scaffolded interior like the casts of circulatory systems on display in the Hunterian Museum. Except that rather than following the shape of a human body, these tendrils were hatched at right-angled horizontals and verticals, filling the void between rectangular walls and a bizarre skeleton only vaguely discernible within. A few years later, and coinciding with my increasing preoccupation with the presence of the nineteenth century within formations of the present, the shell was finally cracked open.

A seated colossus sits upon a structure that is part throne, part plinth. He is depicted in outlandish ceremonial clothing, with the effect of making him look like something out of a superhero comic. The impact is made all the more dramatic as the figure and the base upon which he rests are gold. It is an extraordinary sight. Looking out over an endless flow of traffic, he faces south, high above onlookers and passersby. He is an unearthly giant in a scene of distorted scales. He looms above us, but is himself seated beneath a soaring pinnacle. The figures that surround him also shift according to their own registers of size and proportion, the only certainty is that he is unrivalled in stature. His pose is assertive yet contemplative. It is a depiction of a thoughtful, responsible steward of power. This flattery is extraordinary, considering the unstable, inconsistent nature of the feelings shown to this man in life. He was not always popular, but in death attracted a focused demand for his eternal aggrandizement.

Everything about the structure in which Albert sits is built to support, envelop, cover, elevate, protect and expose him. This is not just architecture in the service of sculpture, but rather it forms an elaborately interdependent structure of affinities: correspondences that convey a narrative of materiality. In his hand is a huge golden book. This is a depiction of the catalogue of the Great Exhibition of the Works and Industry of all Nations. The Great Exhibition ran from May to October 1851, and was housed in a vast iron and glass construction, known as the Crystal Palace, which itself transformed the future of modernity's built environments.

This brief event was the first international exhibition and the largest public visual spectacle then to be staged in the modern world. It framed an international trade and production competition leading to an unprecedented display which I would argue helped forge western modernity's formations of display, spectacle, surveillance and commodity. This helped to determine the form of the modern museum and gallery as well as spaces of commerce, denying any possibility of conceptually separating these sites. This assertion is aligned to what sociological historian Tony Bennett describes as the exhibitionary complex, an arrangement of institutional forms that are museological, but also encompass modes of public spectacle, and sites of commodity arrangement and exchange:

(...) the Great Exhibition of 1851 brought together an

ensemble of disciplines and techniques of display that had been developed within the previous histories of museums, panoramas, Mechanics Institute exhibitions, art galleries, and arcades. In doing so, it translated these into exhibitionary forms which, in simultaneously ordering objects for public inspection and ordering the public that inspected, were to have a profound and lasting influence on the subsequent development of museums, art galleries, expositions, and departments stores. (Bennett 1996, p.83)

The placing of the catalogue in Albert's hand is in recognition of both the significance of the Albert's role in bringing about the Great Exhibition, and of the prominence of this extraordinary event as his primary legacy. In 1850, at the planning stages, Albert was appointed president of the Royal Commission for the Exhibition of 1851, and remained as the public face of the Exhibition, beyond his death and into eternity.

However, this assertive conflation of Albert with the Great Exhibition then leads to a question: Why is his memorial not placed on the nearby actual site of the Crystal Palace in Hyde Park? Answering this necessitates a second question: Why does the statue of Albert not look towards the site of the Great Exhibition? The location of the memorial in Kensington Gardens is to allow for Albert to look down towards the most concrete manifestation of his legacy, which had adopted its informal designation of Albertopolis within his own lifetime. The issue of location is therefore a straightforward one to resolve. 86 acres of land were bought by the Royal Commission for the Exhibition, an organisation formed to oversee the initial event, but that was kept together in order to make use of the enormous profits generated. This land is situated directly to the south of Kensington Gardens, and was the nearest available stretch of property on which to build what became known as Albertopolis. Today, Albert's legacy can be seen amongst the complex of institutions that stand beneath his gaze, and that were built in the metaphorical shadow of the Crystal Palace: the Victoria and Albert Museum, The Science Museum, The Natural History Museum and Imperial College. However, the growth of institutions in this area was as much do to anxiety brought about by a lack of favourable comparison in the international show, as it was by any notions of progressive optimism. A general but dire shortcoming was identified by holding Britain's material culture up to that of the rest of the world as it was represented. The South Kensington Museum was a concrete manifestation of the need to respond to this. Albert gazes out across his legacy, set in motion during his lifetime, unfolding further after death. His field of vision takes in a line of domes and rooftops, running from the Royal Albert Hall, the enigmatic Queen's Tower that stands in the ground of Imperial College, across the Science Museum to the terracotta excesses of the Natural History Museum.

Until recently, the Albert Memorial could have been viewed as a decaying ruin whose crumbling structure embodied the apparently outmoded values of a previous age. As a fossil from the nineteenth century, the memorial is a peculiar and unsettling object to read. This perspective suggests a view through the lens of Walter Benjamin's *Passagen-Werk*, or *Arcades Project*(1999). This is to see it as an 'ur-form', a component object that constitutes an influence, as a form of origin, upon the present historical moment in which it is encountered. For Benjamin, it was the potential aspect of a political education that interested him the most in such objects and sites. The arcades of Paris, the height of newness and fashion in the first half of the 19th century, were the site of petrified ur-forms when Benjamin encountered them in the 1920s and 1930s. They were decaying ruins of a previous epoch of modernity, the embodiment of fashion's transience.

In contrast, the Albert Memorial has been and continues to be a site of restoration, the focus of an enormous cost of time and money. The complication that arises here is that the Albert Memorial is not merely a restored object. As a totality, it had never been in this condition before. In 1872, the memorial was officially inaugurated and its architect George Gilbert Scott was knighted. By 9 March 1876, when the giant golden statue of Albert that we see today was fully realised, in place and unveiled, the structure's white marble, jewels and gold had already been significantly tarnished, stained and dulled by London's corrosive atmosphere. Then within decades, the figure of Albert himself had lost his sheen, gradually darkening and ultimately covered in black paint as an apparent precaution against his visibility as a landmark during enemy air raids. Deteriorating before it was even completed; the precise status of the memorial has been made more obscure by the effort in making it look like new. In a sense, the memorial, in its gleaming, structurally secure and complete form was a new object, even a simulacrum, whose shine has an unreal quality.

As a memorial situated in Kensington Garden, this excessive object is not alone. Nearby, plaques are embedded into paths as a monument for a royal death, to solidify and commemorate the public enactment of bereavement and grief that took place in 1997 after Princess Diana's fatal accident. An existing playground in Kensington Gardens was remade as the Diana, Princes of Wales Memorial Playground, while across the road in Hyde Park is the Diana, Princess of Wales Memorial Fountain. While itself a unique and unexpected event, there was something of an uncanny repetition in this irrepressible need to address a death of significant resonance. Diana's most enduring image of memorial - that of innumerable bunches of flowers, candles, cards and sentimental gifts laid outside Kensington Palace - took as its precedent the fairly recent phenomenon of impromptu roadside shrines that mark the sites of fatal accidents or murders. The degree of expenditure focused at this temporary memorial was hard to not view as an excessive and confusing display. Similarly, it is incontestable that responses to Diana's death were ubiquitous and unavoidable. Much of London, if not the country, ground to a halt on the day of the funeral. There was afterwards a public demand, voiced and articulated by broadcast and print media, that demanded an appropriate and lasting memorial.

These events can be read as a repetition. When the death of Prince Albert was announced *The Times* dramatised the news by framing its columns in black. Conspicuous mourning crossed social and class based boundaries. Prior to the funeral, the wearing of black ribbons was common, and on the day of the funeral itself, the Lord Mayor of London declared a suspension of business in the capital. Such public displays of mourning were soon replaced by an anxiety regarding the inadequacy and unsuitability of temporary or provincial memorials. A burgeoning demand for a permanent and fitting tribute to the Prince Consort became impossible to ignore, fuelled by populist newspaper debates. The eventual outcome was the elaborate architectural and sculptural framework that surrounds the giant golden statue of Albert in Kensington Gardens.

Albert died in the Blue Room at Windsor Castle on Saturday 14 December 1861, aged 42, of typhoid fever. Utilising multiple strategies, Victoria took the form of an embodied memorial to her husband for the rest of her life, still recording the date of his birthday in her journal as late as 1900. On 18 December 1861, Victoria selected the site for the Royal Mausoleum at Frogmore. The building was ready to receive Albert's body a year after his death, but it took another decade to complete the decoration. The Queen simultaneously converted the Wolsey Chapel at St George's, Windsor, into the Albert Memorial Chapel. These examples are the expression of a personal cult of commemoration that included the commissioning of statues and portraits for royal palaces as well as photographs and paintings of herself alongside busts of her husband. Victoria also gave plaster casts of his hands as gifts to their children, and the rooms in where Albert had worked were preserved as if still occupied, as was the room in which he died.

In addition to seeing over 25 commemorative statues in the period following his death, a variety of institutions - orphanages, asylums, schools and hospitals - took Albert's name. Yet these did not address the idea of a definitive, absolute monument. William Cubitt, the Lord Mayor of London, called a public meeting at the Mansion House on 14 January 1862 to instigate the process of constructing a national monument and to establish a committee to raise funds. The money was to be at the disposal of the Queen. The commentary in newspapers tended towards suggestions of historicist-style architectural imitations of grand columns, classical mausoleums and obelisks. The location of the proposed memorial was moved from Hyde Park to the adjacent Kensington Gardens, to facilitate a potentially expanded scheme that could include an institution with some kind of utility value. Henry Cole suggested an Albert University, offering degrees in sciences and arts, but this educational wing of his embryonic museological project in South Kensington was to remain unrealised.

In May 1862, seven architects, whose selection revealed a classical bias, were asked to advise on the project. Thomas Leverton Donaldson, William Tite, Sydney Smirke, James Pennethorne, Matthew Digby Wyatt, Philip Charles Hardwick and George Gilbert Scott. In June the group recommended that in order to contextualise the memorial, that the Kensington Road be straightened, and that a public hall be built to the south of the road - although the combined nature of these two projects was to remain unrealised The seven architects were invited to submit proposals which would encompass the memorial, the immediate surroundings and the public hall for the memorial and its surroundings. The brief dictated that the architecture of the memorial should be primarily a means of setting an effective arrangement of sculpture, particularly the statue of Albert that was to be the centrepiece for any proposal. The positions, dimensions and materials of these sculptures should be indicated without anticipating or interfering with the sculptors' work. The Queen made an initial selection, stating that: 'there were only 2 that would do at all, and only one that is really applicable', namely Hardwick's (Stamp 2000, p.99). The other was Scott's. In May 1863, after some initial resistance, countered by Scott's assertion that Albert himself favoured the gothic style, which unlike obelisks and columns had a particularly Christian character, the Queen approved Scott's gothic design for a monument.

From the invited architects, Scott was the only one associated

with gothic revival. This was a set of ideas that looked to a medieval past, but unlike the historicist reiterations of popular forms of classical and renaissance style as exemplified by the other monument proposals gothic was a tradition of modernity which constructed a past and a set of traditions for itself. Charles Barry's New Palace of Westminster (1837-67) had established gothic revivalism in Britain as a prominent form of the architectural language of government, one based on a constructed historical trajectory. Through the established continuity of an order of legitimate authority, specifically relating to an idealised version of the medieval and the continuation of a tradition of gothic, architectural form could be made to read as an embodiment of patriotic national values relating to religion, learning, law and freedom. Replacing the parliament building which had been destroyed by fire in 1834, the new palace was a demonstration of the ability to use gothic to remake the past itself by remaking its buildings. The decoration of the New Palace of Westminster was overseen by Augustus Welby Pugin, who in the 1830s crystallised the symbolic power and urgency latent in gothic revivalist architecture. He advocated the conflation of structure and symbolic function, which he believed was inherent in medieval architecture: 'A pinnacle, to take one example, is both 'mystical and natural', its verticality making it 'an emblem of the Resurrection', while it is simultaneously 'an upper weathering, to throw off the rain' (Cited in Brooks 1999, pp.9-10).

The linguistic units of gothic revival must also be acknowledged as counterparts to literary sensibilities, which may be less concerned with political and social continuities, and instead offer indulgent spaces of fantasy. This is not meant as a trivialisation of either gothic narratives or spaces of fantasy in general. Rather it is meant to emphasise another dimension to architectural forms, as projections and articulations of fantasy, itself a form of material and social considerations. The oppositions to gothic might follow exactly such a distinction. A mythically constructed sense of classicism as an embodiment of a sophisticated rationalism could easily present its inverse in the medieval atavism of gothic. The sense of gothic as atavism pervaded as a counter argument, a fearful response to an irrational and outmoded form that seemed not only decadent and impractical, but degenerate. Yet gothic architecture also offered an affinity with meditative qualities. Melancholy reflections, the image of a figure solitarily contemplating medieval ruins, tropes also associated with the sublime, were tropes of both gothic tendencies emerging in eighteenth century literature and were compatible with gothic's revived architectural forms. The scale of the literary and visual imagination implicated here is great, but perhaps this overlap is revealed most usefully and efficiently here by a popular sub-genre of eighteenth century gothic, a loosely constituted group, including Thomas Parnell, Robert Blair and Thomas Gray, known as the Graveyard Poets.

For Joseph Addison, writing in *The Spectator* in 1711, gothic spaces of gloominess are not purely sites of indulgent melancholy. They are presented as opportunities for instructive thoughtfulness, albeit with a tendency for the straightforward morality of the *vanitas*:

> I know that Entertainments of this Nature, are apt to raise dark and dismal Thoughts in timorous Minds and gloomy Imaginations; but for my Part, though I am always serious, I do not know what it is to be melancholy; and can therefore take a View of Nature in her deep and solemn Scenes, with the same Pleasure as her most gay and delightful ones. By this Means I can improve my self with those Objects which other consider with Terrour. (Addison 2006, p.189)

A similar instructiveness is present in Robert Blair's *The Grave* (1743), which evokes imagery of rising spectres and an overwhelming horror of the tomb, yet urges readers to be wary of straying from the path of Godliness. Horror has an ethical purpose, offering redemption and guidance.

Yet between the emergence of these forms of literary gothic at the beginning of the eighteenth century, and its dark apotheosis at the end of the nineteenth century, the relationship between narrative fiction and architectural discourse can be read as one of increasing estrangement. The space of sensation and transgression becomes a point of divergence from literary and architectural gothic. While those elements are present in the architectural forms they are overwhelming in a manner that suggests an alignment with the sublime while gothic as a literary form moves further away from an explicit agenda of edification. In its fictional dimension, gothic snowballed as an indulgently exploitative dramatisation of degeneration. Fin de Siècle gothic - a term given focus by Kelly Hurley (1996) - should also be read as a critical force. Perhaps not as a form of guidance, but as a challenge to normative boundaries in which excess and uncertainty flow out of all control, demanding acts of rethinking social and subjective constitution. However, perhaps it is possible to reach an alternative supposition: The Albert Memorial is itself an excessive form, transgressing boundaries both within its own temporal context, and as a remainder. Inscriptions of clear intention and legibility now haunt the present as a shimmering and uncertain spectre.

Indeed, the contestation of gothic as an appropriate form of architecture may also reflect a perceived threat to the order and stability embodied in classicist designs. The place of gothic revival as a contender for architecture of state was not uncontested, and at the time of Scott's monumental proposal, there were few prevalent examples of recent gothic buildings in Britain. Scott himself was pressured into abandoning his gothic design for the Foreign Office in Whitehall (1856-9), for which he substituted a scheme in the renaissance style. His plan for Albert's monument, however, would see no such compromise:

The idea which I have worked out may be described as a colossal statue of the Prince, placed beneath a vast and magnificent shrine or tabernacle, and surrounded by works of sculpture illustrating those arts and sciences which he fostered, and the great undertakings which he originated. I have, in the first place, elevated the Monument upon a lofty and wide-spreading pyramid of steps. From the upper platform rises a Podium or continuous pedestal, surrounded by sculptures in alto-relievo, representing historical groups or series of the most eminent artists of all ages of the world: the four sides being devoted severally to Painting, Sculpture, Architecture, Poetry and Music. (...) Besides the sculpture already described as surrounding the Podium, there are on pedestals projecting from each of its angles, groups illustrating the industrial arts of Agriculture, Manufactures, Commerce, and Engineering. Above these, against the pillars, and also in the angles of the gables, are statues which represent the greater sciences, and in the tabernacle-work of the spire are figures of angels and of the Christian virtues. (Scott 1872, pp.9-10)

As well as offering a device to protect and emphasise the statue of Albert, Scott's design had an odd quality of modernity about it. It was a recently revived form in European architecture, yet takes as its precedent medieval forms. He was influenced by recent designs from Germany, particularly by the work of Karl Frederick Schinkel and Christian Daniel Rausch, as well as by Pugin. Yet there are realised architectural precedents for the memorial that Scott identified, most notably the Eleanor Crosses. In 1840, Scott had made studies of the surviving Eleanor crosses at Geddington, Northampton and Waltham. These had been erected by Edward I at sites where Queen Eleanor's body had rested on its journey from Nottinghamshire to London. However, although drawing upon his knowledge of medieval architecture, Scott attempted to stress a sense of originality distinct from medieval influences, based upon a scale intended to emphasise the importance of the subject matter and a structural specificity of function.

There was another particular quality to the shrine that Scott favoured. He described these shrines as

> (...) imaginary buildings, such as had never in reality been
> erected; and my idea was to realise one of these imaginary
> structures with its precious metals, its inlaying, its enamels,
> etc., etc. This was an idea so new, as to provoke much
> opposition. (Stamp, p.102)

That Scott took as his precedent for his structures a form of
architecture that was ancient, yet suggestive of a previously
unrealised fantasy, signifies something other than a reductive
historicism in their conception. To translate these fairy-like
forms into actuality was to aim for a type of building that had
never existed before. The use of a style of building that did not
necessarily exist is echoed by the present form of the memorial,
restored to a condition that never existed prior to restoration.
The gothic style provided a resistance to an established tradition
of language and reference in architectural practice. The
historian Chris Brooks has pointed out, with reference to the
construction of gothic as a fantasised medieval source, that
'modernity could only create itself by also creating a past from
which the present was different' (Brooks 1999, p.18). Yet any
sense of modernity was also based on ideas relating to
construction itself. Of paramount importance to Scott's interest
in medieval architecture was that it offered lessons in building,
especially in relation to integrity towards the architectural
elements that it included. Gothic was a system of architecture
for Scott, one that could be applied with a degree of flexibility
and invention, a system that could absorb new materials and
innovative practices without risk its integrity or authority.
Gothic also offered an ideal of a collaborative approach to
making buildings. This was the job of architects, engineers and
sculptors, and incorporated an even broader range of craft skills
and traditions.

If this process was the realisation of the gothic revival as a bringing together of the skills of many disciplines, it is still thecase that this memorial privileges sculpture. The sculpture was conceived of as a set of clearly articulated signs serving unambiguously didactic gestures. A handbook published in 1874 provided a detailed guide, with no ambiguity of intention, to the elaborate iconography of the memorial. The idealised aspirations of Victoria's reign were to be summarised, but within this the position of Albert was paramount. He was to be situated as a paragon, providing cohesion between continents, and overseeing a linear history of knowledge represented by commerce, manufacture, engineering and fine arts, that finds its focused culmination embodied in Albert himself. On a series of four pedestals, one at each corner of the steps, are a group of sculptures that are perhaps more prominent when walking around the memorial than the golden figure of Albert. These could be seen as the most problematic aspect of an encounter with the memorial, both in respect to their prominence and their subject matter. They depict race and nationality in terms defined by Imperial Britain. Politically they are volatile representations to defend, as they have been defended against damage through conservation. Each pedestal represents one of four groups 'allegorically relating to the four quarters of the globe and their productions: thus referring indirectly to the International Exhibition of 1851' (Handbook 1874, p.10). This was an intended representational form referring to an earlier form of representation, the Great Exhibition, as a means of Victoria's nation defining the world in relation to itself, while simultaneously transforming that world. These are all very problematic depictions, but I would like to draw attention to the group representing Asia, by the sculptor John Henry Foley. It is described in the 1874 Handbook:

In this group the central figure alone is a female. She is seated on an elephant, and the action of removing her veil is an allusion to the important display of the products of Asia, which was made at the Great Exhibition of 1851. (1874, p.13)

That the same interpretation of this figure, arranged in a passive and objectified display of her body as a means of representing India as a key imperial territory, should appear without comment in 1981 in a work by Stephen Bayley, one of only a few published historical contextualisations, is all the more confusing in terms of approaching the memorial (1981, p.55). As a way of engaging with this difficult object, I would like to consider how the memorial may be read as an artefact of material culture, but also as a form of text. A useful approach to material culture is provided by Preziosi and Hitchcock in their study of the Bronze Age Aegean. Preziosi and Hitchcock write:

...with the understanding that the visual and material cultures of a society (...) constitute forms of individual and social technologies or instruments for the active construction, maintenance, and transformation of individual and social realities. (1999, p.25)

These visual and material cultures, as they are described, include what might be accounted for today in terms of art and architecture. Material culture, as it might be described, is read as much as a set of active social processes as it is a set of objects or built environments. Although such things as objects and architecture may by the very things that are read in close detail, it is not a process of framing them as reflection, trace or the residue of social activities. Preziosi and Hitchcock also stress the need to question the sequential order of such an assumption, that in deliberately not reading objects as reflections of ideas, attitudes or mentalities is the recognition that such acceptably social forms do not precede any form of material expression in which they are given long lasting form. Implied is a sense of mutual interdependence between, on the one hand, the construction of social forms and modes of identity and, on the other, forms of objects that do not only serve as representative shadows of the former, but are active forms of their constitution. That they remain after their living culture has ceased to exist is misleading if it gives the impression that they were not a living part of it.

The approach put forward here is situated between two perspectives of reading objects as surviving fragments of the past. One side of the division is determined by the assumption that an object's meaning is fixed as an imprint of the intention of its makers. These are likened to the physical and chemical properties of an object which are retained, fixed and readable. The task of the reader is then one of deduction and reconstruction of original intentions. An object of this kind of analysis becomes analogous to a 'text', with the use forming a 'con-text'. This object/context relationship is privileged in this model, as the only legitimate source of interpretation, which is to be executed by the relevant expert. The metaphor here is a distinctly modern one in which the object is analogous to a medium of communication. Ideas or values move from maker or maker's society through to an attendant viewer or reader in the present. This is a model that also privileges the role and function of the trained expert who can stand as sanctioned interpreter. Yet on the other hand this is a mode of thought that might be held up as the opposite to the one just described: 'the notion that the meaning of an object is entirely or largely in the eyes and imagination of its beholders or users'(Preziosi and Hitchcock 1999, p.26).

What is described here is a compatible and simultaneous plausibility of apparently antagonistic positions. Preziosi and Hitchcock describe this situation as being made available by the relative permanence that artefacts display:

(…) they remain to be used and reused, and thought about in potentially new and possibly quite unforseen or unintended ways over time – unlike a spoken utterance, which materially disappears unless it is recorded. (1999, p.26)

It is the endurance of things that allows them to be read outside of their original conditions, while still retaining varying degrees of that originary context and meaning. The mode of analysis that Preziosi and Hitchcock lay out here recognises the limitations of adhering either to a pure model of holding that an object's significance is embodied within the object itself, or to one that dictates that meaning can only be found in the perception of the viewer. By granting that both seemingly irreconcilable positions are not only plausible, but necessarily compatible, their position allows for readings that acknowledge original intentions and function, while recognising the likely impossibility of any such meanings being fully reconstructed. Perhaps even more significant is the facilitation of interpretations that are not only multiple, but perhaps conflicting and antagonistic. This position is one that is usefully contextualized by a Derridean description of authorship which sees the reliance of any inscription of meaning through a medium upon a culturally specific system of language. This system cannot be dominated or controlled by an author. The attentive and critical act of reading, both as phenomenological and hermeneutic act, must therefore be one that looks for relationships between what an author does or does not command. It is reading, therefore, that enables the production of a signifying structure of interpretation around the object(Derrida 1997, p.158). In an object such as the memorial, shifting authorial, hermeneutic and temporal layers concatenate within the dimensions of the encounter.

The reading of material culture can be expanded beyond these terms. Christopher Tilley has made a case for modes of analysing material culture, both in anthropological and archaeological contexts, with reference to text:

> Material culture is 'written' through a practice of spacing and differentiation in just the same manner as phonetic writing. Both result in the material fixation of meaning which, by contrast to speech, is indirectly communicated in the sense that I decorate a pot by dividing up the empty space of the clay or write a letter by inscribing marks on a blank sheet of paper and at some time in the future you read and interpret the visual medium, able by virtue of the material fixation to read what I have produced. (1991, pp.16-17)

Text and material culture involve transformations that affect spacing, differentiation and articulation. Both are structured through spatial ordering and distinction, and the articulation of units of difference. While there are shared structural properties between text and material culture, and also speech, Tilley is also clear on the obviousness of difference and incompatibility:

> However, as everyone knows, to make even the simplest statement such as 'It is raining' with material objects would be rather difficult. In fact it would be a complete waste of time and effort. (1991, p.17)

The meanings constituted by material culture are not communicated forms of meaning content in this sense. Communicative statements through the articulations of material culture are better thought of as analogous. However, Tilley's textual metaphors are tame. He recognises a structuralist grammar of things, and a poststructuralist emphasis on metaphors of text. Yet he fails to grasp Derrida's sense of writing and différance. Language is ultimately bound to a predominantly structuralist understanding of it as a series of differential units. A more complete recognition of the extent to which arche-writing is something without discursive exterior would serve Tilley more fully here, and allow the erasing of such a well-defined boundary between text and material culture. Even so, a reading of Tilley illuminates the space between text and material culture as traversable and bi-directional. There are also implications for disciplines themselves. Specifically, archaeology could be described as consisting of textualization. In short, this description applies to the need to conceive of material culture as an archaeological world through the use of language, making objects intelligible through their transference of transformation into words, as Bjornar Olsen suggests:

> In short, archaeology is text, and to realize that we participate in the same structure as the epic, the novel and the drama is to let out own practice as producer of this text be examined by the same procedures as those applied to literary texts. (1990, p.164)

Within this assertion of material culture's discursive field as one that is text is a possibility of reading memorial objects.

The possibility that a nuanced reading of material culture as text offers is suggestive of acts of responsible and engaged acts of reading. It is in these terms that I would like to consider the Albert Memorial. The act of writing, or in this case the inscription of meaning through architecture and sculpture, relies upon a culturally specific system of language that cannot be dominated by an author. A critical reading must look for a relationship between what an author does or does not command, therefore enabling the production, through reading, of a signifying structure. In its unveiled form, it provides a brashly conspicuous focal point for visitors to the park, an object that is excessive in its visibility. Yet the kinds of encounters that are made available by this monument are not clear, particularly due to the depth of contextual specificity. It is tied to a series of very particular, codified intentionalities, but the readability of the memorial slips further and further into obscurity, and the imagery starts to look inappropriate in an object that stands for national values. Yet this is an object that has been subject to enormous investment - at a cost of £11.25 million - and that is a prominent feature upon London's landscape. This problem manifests itself as a question of archaic ideology and how to address historical forms of representation as they exist in the present. If this is an origin for a contemporary form of modernity in Britain, how is it to be read and by whom? The memorial, as a simulacral fossil, is an object of beauty and fascination. Simultaneously, to encounter it suggests

an ambiguity surrounding it as a site of ideological representation in a country that is attempting to come to terms with its post-colonial status and responsibilities. However, the use of gothic provided an opportunity to define a sense of modernity through the construction of a past from which the present could be differentiated. Since its conservation it is possible to read the memorial as a form of new - or remade - object, analogous to the ability of Gothic Revival architecture to symbolically remake the meanings of the past, and the subsequent definition of the present, by remaking its objects.

Chapter 2

The Beasts of Sydenham

Following the southward direction of Albert's gaze for seven miles or so, albeit with some eastwards drift, leads to the final resting place of Joseph Paxton's Crystal Palace, where it stood in a reconfigured form until destroyed by fire in 1936. The decaying terraces and balustrades of Crystal Palace Park today might register as an obscure historical footnote, a melancholy suburban anomaly that risks being effaced by the ongoing transformation of London's geography. The Park and its ruins do not convey the scale and impact of the Crystal Palace, or the influence that this dream world has had on our contemporary psychic and material environment. The Great Exhibition, as a fixed point in time, overshadows the afterlife of the Crystal Palace, yet these remains anchor the present in that moment, while illuminating a passage of singular importance in their own terms.

As agreed in the initial terms of the Great Exhibition's approval, the building was dismantled and the Hyde Park site restored. Paxton was part of a consortium set up to make use of profits generated by the Exhibition to buy the building from the contractors who built it. These funds also enabled the purchase of a 200-acre wooden parkland, located on the summit of Sydenham Hill. Of this location, Samuel Phillips gives an account in his Guide to the Crystal Palace Park from 1856:

> The Crystal Palace stands in the county of Surrey, immediately on the confines of Kent, bordered on one side by Sydenham, and on the other by Norwood and Anerly, whilst Penge lies at the foot of the hill, and Dulwich Wood at the top. No particular topographical or historical facts are associated with these places. (Phillips 1856, p.29)

Once relocated, the life of the Crystal Palace could now be extended indefinitely. The lack of budgetary restrictions and spatial limitations allowed the building to mutate far beyond the scale of Hyde Park. The glass surface area was doubled, and the form elaborately refashioned. The rebuilding began in 1852 and was completed in 1854, during which time the grounds in Sydenham were transformed into an enormous landscaped park. To power an expansive circulatory system of fountains Isambard Kingdom Brunel designed a pair of towers to stand at either side of the building. Paxton and his consortium envisaged a spectacular environment, buying trees, plants and flowers that would populate the landscape and pass through the glass walls into an internal winter garden. Throughout the grounds were laid out a maze, a grotto, a rosary, groves, temples, lawns, lakes and islands. Material was gathered to fill the internal sculpture courts with casts, as well as to ornament the external terrace. The statuary was drawn from a broad base to chronicle an idealised account of European sculpture as an apotheosis of Western civilization.

Inside the central transept was Follet Osler's Crystal Fountain – 27 feet high and made from four tons of crystal glass - which had been a star exhibit of the 1851 exhibition. From there, running down the north nave was a series of courts laying out for a visiting public the embryonic discourse of 'The History of Art', each one a stop along a particular period in time and style. Another star exhibit from Hyde Park, Pugin's Mediaeval Court, had been put on display elsewhere in the Crystal Palace, inspiring an entire series of related simulacra. It was placed in a teleological sequence which included courts of categorised styles: Grecian and Roman, Assyrian, Egyptian – which contained sphinxes, towering colossi, obelisks, and fake mummies - Byzantine, Romanesque, ancient Chinese, Renaissance. These were appended with a recreation of a house disinterred from the ruins of Pompeii and a version of the Alhambra. Architecture, mural decoration and sculpture were laid out in a visually spectacular sequence leading to the sixteenth century so that the visitor:

> (...) might gain, in practical fashion, an idea of the successive stages of civilisation which have from time to time arisen in the world, have changed or sunk into decadence, have been violently overthrown, or have passed away, by the aggressions of barbarians, or the no less degrading agency of sensual and enervating luxury. (Beaver 1993, p.84)

The order here asserted the permanence and superiority of the British Empire casting all else as transient, a teleology culminating in the current order. This impermanence reflected European prejudices of non-western societies, either as home to once great but now decadent, degraded cultures, or as examples of 'primitive' antecedents. The progressive development of the courts, focusing on the fountain as an apex, makes an unambiguous affirmation of temporal progress. There are evolutionary and temporal implications evoked here that reverberate across the park to the extent that a deep and contested set of narratives of temporality determine the resonant frequency of the ruins of the Crystal Palace.

Inside there were also displays of thousands of natural history specimens which included displays of various ethnographic groups of people: 'Life like and life sized groups of Bushmen,

Zulu, Kaffir, Mexican Indian, Hindoos, Tibetans etc. with zoological and botanical specimens of the several countries' (Bell-Knight 1976, p.66). This horrific display turned people into crude, racially categorised, signifiers that were equivalent to the trophies and curiosities of natural history, hunting and colonial domination. A level of equivalence was achieved between the actual, preserved, bodies of animals as items of display, and convincing replicas of people. The notion of a distinction between authentic and replica, as with all the displays in and around the Crystal Palace, is never implied.

Also contained within the Crystal Palace was a tropical department which included Paxton's favourite lily. This was the Victoria Regia lily, for which Paxton designed a glasshouse at Chatsworth, Derbyshire. In 1849, his daughter – Annie Paxton – demonstrated the structural strength of its leaf by sitting upon one in its water tank. The underside of the leaf inspired the two way spanning structural rib system of the lily house and subsequently of the Crystal Palace. There was an orangery and also a monkey house, adding to the impression of a tropical biosphere to withstand the English climate. There was a gallery of old and contemporary paintings, a carriage department providing an assortment of approved styles. It also contained an extensive library and reading room, a court of kings and queens, a hall of fame, a theatre, a concert room with 4000 seats and a Grand Orchestra built around a giant organ with over 4500 pipes. There was an area described as a museum, which specialised in raw materials for food, industrial and craft based production from around the world. There were photographic facilities for public and professional use, a school of art, which incorporated lessons in science, literature, geography at elementary and advanced levels. Furthermore, lessons in decorative art, university style lectures in English and German literature and general history were available, in addition to a school of engineering, a music school, secondary schools and departments for catering and refreshment. A tradition of various side shows had also been established at an early stage.

The human activity and physical geography that surrounded these ruins was as much an element of the spectacular display as any of the objects in the Great Exhibition. The museological form of the exhibition hall has a greater scope than the notion of the displaying of portable or confinable objects. The artefact of material culture is, as Susan M. Pearce suggests, expandable to the extent that 'the whole of cultural expression, one way or another, falls within the realm of material culture'. (1996, p.9) As material culture, this becomes potential museum material, as does a more conventionally scaled 'thing' or 'specimen':

> Strictly speaking, the lumps of the physical world to which cultural value is ascribed include not merely those discrete lumps capable of being moved from one place to another (...) but also the larger physical world of landscape with all the social structure that it carries, the animal and plant species which have been affected by humankind (and most have), the prepared meals which the animals have become, and even the manipulation of flesh and air which produces song and speech. (Pearce 1996, p.9)

This is a vital concept in the understanding of the outlook of the new Crystal Palace: it was looking upon the visible domain as its own spectacle, and therefore as included within its own narratives. The panoramic landscape and all that it contained was held in the discourse of the display. This was unprecedented on such a scale as a public, commercial, entertainment. The sprawling, expansive and mutated nature of the new Crystal Palace was reflective of this attempt to encompass as much as possible. The technology of the panoramic display at Sydenham is that of selection, which the technology of the museological manifests. All can be brought into the realm of material culture, as through selection and display it becomes part of the world of human values. This is a process that works against the romantic, sublime notion of landscape in which the subject is encompassed by infinite scale which cannot be comprehended. Instead, the appearance of the sublime is rendered as a controlled attraction or entertainment.

During its first thirty years, the Crystal Palace received an average of 2,000,000 visitors per year. Two new railway lines were built to facilitate the huge numbers of visitors, creating a profound influence on the shaping and development of South London as a whole. As well as the addition of the huge marine aquarium in 1872 an enormous zoetrope was opened in 1868. Powered by a gas engine, this provided the first mass audience with examples of moving images. As well as the regular attraction of balloon ascents, there were all manner of temporary events, such as rose shows, dog shows, poultry shows, in addition to trade fairs and various kinds of arts, crafts and industrial exhibition. It was commonly used as a meeting place for thousands of large organisations. There were also numerous concerts, music festivals, circuses and pantomimes.

One of the Crystal Palace's speciality events was the holding of vast and elaborate fireworks displays. Yet these were overshadowed by the extravagant spectacle of John M. East's Invasion, each performance drawing at least 25,000 spectators. On the open space in front of the terraces a full-sized village had been built in great detail, inhabited by a crowd of actors, complete with carriages and horses and a regiment of ersatz soldiers. The village was then attacked by an overhead Zeppelin, dropping bombs on the school and the church, before invading troops parachuted down onto the village leading to a full-scale battle on the ground. The ruined village had then to be reconstructed for every performance. The Palace also had a great symbolic importance in its first 30 years. For example, in 1872, Disraeli gave a speech promoting the empire as central to the Conservative party, utilising the site as both a representation of the nation and empire.

However, the popularity of the site began to wane towards the end of the century. Entropic forces rivalled the seductive allure of progress. Competition from seaside resorts played a significant part in this decline, drawing crowds away with the promise of a different kind of space, in which visitors could experience both the spatial alterity of sea and promenade, as well as a less stratified social space, in which classes interacted across boundaries, and that offered both symbolic and actual transgressions. The growth of railways, so important in supplying the Crystal Palace with its source of visitors, had now enabled ever increasing numbers to escape towards outposts of pleasure and recreation, propelled by an overall increase in national earnings. The seeking of new pleasures lured crowds away from a Palace that had started to lose its shine. Although in 1904 *The Times* newspaper likened the Crystal Palace to an illustrated encyclopaedia of the universe, it was by this stage in financial crises.

In 1911, the site was the venue for the 'Festival of Empire', in the year of King George V's Coronation. The British Empire was constructed in miniature, including timber and plaster three-quarter-size replicas of the parliament buildings of all the Commonwealth countries. Exhibitions of the products of each country were displayed inside. A miniature railway toured the empire. Stops included a South African diamond mine, an Indian tea plantation and jungle, with wild animals, a Malay village and a Canadian logging camp. This was the biggest show ever put on there but it could not save the Crystal Palace from bankruptcy and closure. The building was sold but then bought to become the property of the Nation. After it was bought by the government, it was used as a naval supply depot during the First World War, leading to further deterioration. It did not reopen until 1920, when one last attempt was made to restore the nearly derelict site. That year, King George V and Queen Mary opened the Imperial War Museum, housed inside the Crystal Palace. Visitors began returning, but in small numbers. The entertainments were less grand than they had been, including brass band competitions and beauty pageants. A large part of the gardens had been converted into a race track. The building was rusting and decaying, the fountains no longer worked and the stonework in the grounds was crumbling. In the years before its destruction by fire in 1936, the Palace had already begun to resemble a ruin of a previous epoch.

The origins of modern display in relation to international exhibitions are dealt with elegantly by Paul Greenhalgh. He points out that the Great Exhibition and its successors did not spring out of nowhere, but rather developed over a period of time in France and Britain. Promoting trade and technological development, political posturing, education and social improvement were all factors at work in the early decades of the nineteenth century. In fact, these activities had been institutionalised in France, by the end of the eighteenth, spurred on by the pressures brought about through revolution and war, but also through the pressure applied by a need to compete with firms from across the Channel, such as Wedgewood. Greenhalgh draws particular attention to the 1789 exhibition on the Champs de Mars. This exhibition demonstrated presentation as marketing, as the generation of confidence, with the aim of the replication of the success of industrialisation in England. The impressive built structures were put into context by staged events:

> A plethora of activity filled the Champs de Mars; there were military parades, splendid balls, firework displays and dozens of unofficial sideshows and stalls on the edge of the site. The strange combinations of carnival and ceremony, of circus and museum, of popularism and elitism which typified the Expositions Universelles therefore emerged in embryonic form at the very opening of the tradition. (Greenhalgh 1988, p.5)

This was followed by half a century of ambitious national exhibitions in France while the Society of the Arts and been doing so on a smaller scale in England.

The tradition of international exhibition that grew out of these beginnings was carried on after the Great Exhibition at South Kensington, within the borders of Albertopolis: from the South Kensington Exhibition of 1862, continuing on the site into the 1880s, while the impression of the form radiated globally. The Crystal Palace was connected to, yet distinct from the model of the international exhibition, as it was not bound by the need to promote industry and technology quite so directly. Instead, it emphasised those aspects through edification and entertainment. It was unique, more importantly, in its permanence. However, permanence can be distorted into a twisted, possibly degenerate form.

At the beginning of the 21st Century, prior to hotly contested redevelopment of the site, it is still possible to walk along the decaying terraces of Crystal Palace Park, which once served as a dramatic foreground for the building, but now stand as ruins. A handful of statues are visible, situated amongst the extensive but structurally unsound balustrades. Their form, makers and subjects have fallen into obscurity. These statues are fossilised clues to the dream world that was the Crystal Palace, yet it is their advanced state of decay that is the most suggestive. At first glance, they resemble an idealised image of classical ruins. However, on closer inspection of the eroded surfaces, it becomes clear that this is concrete, reinforced with rusted metal rods – an adaptation of the Roman invention of concrete as a technology of industrial modernity. Most of the figures have cracked. Open chasms, revealing that they are totally hollow. These ruins appear to be some obscure historical footnote, a melancholic suburban anomaly soon to be effaced by the ongoing transformation of the city's geography. They do not convey the scale and impact of the Crystal Palace, or the influence that this dream world has had on our contemporary psychic and material environment.

Walking the paths and lawns, this place seems to be a pleasure garden, well-used, busy, and lively. Yet it has also contained other activities over the past few years. Part of the site was occupied as an   eco village, while more consistently the park has been home home to a sports ground, swimming pool and concert venue. This variation is consistent with the park's history. It is, and has always been, many things. Yet when approached without direct instrumentality, from an angle other than that of its many functions, a more revealing status becomes visible. It is a science fiction disaster scene. This peculiar quality is related to the sites of alien intervention in Boris and Arkady Strugatsky's *Roadside Picnic* (2007). These Visitation Zones, left behind after some inexplicable happening in which 6 regions are touched by an extraterrestrial presence, are toxic, urban badlands in which only specialised stalkers can navigate, at great risk. Scattered across the barren Zones are incomprehensible artefacts, traces of a culture, of a purpose that it appears impossible to begin to uncover. The order of things is disrupted, creating areas of displacements, anomalies, distortions. Also, perhaps, like the mysterious island in the TV show *Lost*, the park is a distinct region that feels like the rule of normality does not quite apply. There is a strange sense of intensity here, or rather of an intensification of forces. These are forces of history and modernity, of energies and explosions. Having endured the heat of progress, and the actual fire that raised the building, the burnt out remains of the park no longer smoulder, but have been covered in new growth. The park, the entire district that bears the name, has its own life, almost entirely detached from the burden of history. It is the opposite of the 'non-place' as described by Marc Augé(1995). This is a place saturated by the presence of history, not characterised by an alienation to the past, to tradition or continuity. Rather, to borrow from Robert Smithson, it is a non-site (Flam 1996). Its boundaries are spatial, temporal, and porous. It radiates the trace energy of an initial cataclysm. Decades of leakage have spread the Crystal Palace's contaminating influence. The explicit and pedagogical narratives of progress may have lost some of their primacy, but cannot be expunged, cannot be decontaminated. They remain as a background radiation, integrated within the ideological structures of global modernity.

The metaphor of *Roadside Picnic*, which gives the novel its title, is that of ants coming across the strewn remains of said picnic. What these ants are to the absent diners who left scraps of food, paper plates and plastic cups, reflects the status of humans to the alien entities who visited the Earth. However, unlike the zones of *Roadside Picnic*, in which humanity is left traces that are beyond comprehension, the Crystal Palace Park is a site that is more explicit in its comprehension, if only one attends to the traces of narrative. These point to something slow moving, but legible. In *Roadside Picnic*, the protagonists are left to make sense of their own tragic meaningless lives. Here, in contrast, is a chance to explore modernity's own creation myth. To explore the ruins of a lost civilisation that happens to be the one that you probably live in. It is a fragment of a greater part of an explosion, of an event, that like the theoretical model of the big bang leaves its radioactive traces as a background noise to the universe. But this is no process of scientific objectivity, if indeed such a thing can be realistically claimed. Rather, projections are in effect here.

Time travels in different directions at the Crystal Palace settling in loose configurations. Images of the past take form, are frozen, and start to move backwards, but also become more lifeless. Observers peer into the has-been, through veins that overlay the present, exist simultaneously with the now, and the to-come. This perspective, if engaged with, might disrupt the now, peeling away its surfaces. Time can open up as the space of the park does, to investigation, as narrow streets give way to open lawns, pavements to broad paths and walkways. The park itself does not give much away about its past, or at least, it is less than forthcoming about the extent of the narratives that underlie the site. Nor should it particularly, according to the dominant ideological impulses that maintain authority over the park. The contested nature of the site, with its long fought over plans for a radical development, of cinema, leisure centre, shopping mall, mean that Bromley Council may not want to get too attached to the idea that this a place of inalienable historical importance, a site of world heritage, if it is successful in destroying the last traces of it to make way for car parking and oversized sheds for spectacular commodities and commodified spectacles. Such a transformation, however, would not be inappropriate. It is the space of western public space as loosely modelled upon the Palace, without its spirit of instruction and edification, without any morality, but merely a purer form of capital, and a purer form of ideological simplicity.

The contestation has been unresolved for many years now,

with rival interests amongst developers, who see it as a retailing and entertainment complex, local residents, enthusiasts of history and heritage, local authorities. As I write, a recent proposal for a huge scale commercial development is focused upon a full scale facsimile of the building itself, funded purely by commercial means, and incorporating a housing development. There is a twisted integrity to this, and to all the commercial redevelopments. This always was a commercial project. More than this, the initial function of the Crystal Palace, in housing the Great Exhibition, was the creation of an international globalised economy, of free trade and commodities. It would destroy the ruin, but there is a kind oflogic to these projects. Yet it is instrumental logic that is manifested here which is the enemy of materialist enchantment. Development of the site would see the end of the generative ruin, of the fossil, with its clashing planes of identity, as park, wreckage, site of scientific and historic importance, and a place with a great deal of irrational magical power. The transformation looms as perpetually inevitable and immanent, yet deferred, as if by this talismanic power of the site itself. This sense of enchantment runs deeply in the land, is bound by time and tradition, and a history of origins. Crystal Palace is also Crystal World, strangely magical and material.

As a pleasure garden, it was always a modern space. Little has changed in that basic regard. One exception is the visually dramatic stage, a trace of the architectural radicalism that once defined the entire site. This angular structure seems to have learnt much from the monumental cuts in space that sculptor Richard Serra has achieved using huge sheets of steel. The platform-stage built by Ian Ritchie Architects in 1997, looks over a lily pond, echoing Paxton's former role as a builder and keeper of greenhouses, and faces a bowled lawn, an auditorium shaped by the site's curved, sloping topography. However, an overall purpose of pleasurable edification seems now part of the banal sheen of weekend recreation; the park is a space for social time, for strolling, playing. The grand project replaced by leisure as defined by newspaper colour supplements: as a fear of totalities, of an obsession with short term planning, increasing urban privatisation and short term profiteering fills the gaps.

The only objects to survive intact from the 1850s are a group of sculptures occupying a miniature archipelago. Each of these depicts, in painstakingly researched realism, a creature long-extinct, yet shockingly novel. This sense of disorientating and radical newness is difficult to reconstruct. Consequently, it is easy to see the monsters as comical, to dismiss them as mistaken interpretations, and as themselves somewhat primitive in their representational inaccuracies. This, however, is misrecognition of what are extraordinary depictions of both a lost category of life, and of an unprecedented, continuing remaking of the past. It is difficult to imagine a sense of the contemporary without the depth of previously elapsed time that late-modernity now describes, to imagine all of time to have been within the scale of the existence of culturally developed humans. Yet this sense of temporal depth is a factor developed only in the period of early modernity. The 'discovery' of non-biblical time – a chronology distinct from that set out in the Bible – was analogous to the 'invention' of history, and the two were brought together in a spectacular form before a mass audience at Sydenham.

A key factor in the formation of modernity's discourse on time is the fossil. Of the use of fossils as a means of assessing the relative ages of rocks, the palaeontologist Stephen Jay Gould states that 'No issue could be more important in developing a proper methodology for reconstructing history' (1990, p.81). They were a means of satisfying the need for geologists to have a criterion of history. This type of historicism, based on observation and a scientifically methodical practice, can be read as possessing a critical impulse, as it was a means of dispelling both misconception and mythic – religious – dogma. Dogmatic historicism also might here include the erroneous form Social Darwinism targeted by Walter Benjamin's *Arcades Project*: 'Originally, Darwin's theory had a critical impulse (...) But within Social Darwinism, that critical impulse was lost. The idea of social evolution in effect glorified the blind, empirical course of human history'(Buck-Morss 1993, p.58). The idea of the fossil is therefore one with an inherent critical potential within the context of its historical interpretation. For Benjamin, industrial objects from previous eras were viewed as fossils: 'as the trace of living history that can be read from the surfaces of the surviving objects' (Buck-Morss 1993, p.56).

The Crystal Palace Dinosaurs can be read as living fossils, as the surviving objects of another epoch, which, as images of extinct, evolutionarily obsolete phenomena, could only exist as mediated representational forms. The origins of the Crystal Palace Dinosaurs, and the gap between them and those of *Jurassic Park*, offer forms of historical narrative. These mediated representations have the potential to be brought to speech. These dinosaurs are an invention. It is not possible to pin down a singular moment of their invention, rather they can be thought of as born out of rivalry and contestation, the focus of a struggle for both ownership and interpretation. However, the act of naming a public, authoritative inscription can be located and attributed to a credited author. While this comes about as a proprietorial act, the term slips quickly from the hands of the creator, and from his intended interpretation. The author of the term, and therefore the most authoritative claimant for some form of provisional control, is Richard Owen. Owen had been chairman of a panel of judges for the Great Exhibition, and can be viewed as one of the most prominent and significant figures in the field of Victorian natural history. The term came about in 1842 in the writing up of a report for publication of a talk given in August the previous year to the British Association for the Advancement of Science. Between the giving of the talk and the publication of its written form, Owen became convinced that the fossilised remains that had been the subject of his attention belonged to the same group. It made these animals part of a shared category, but also distinct from any extant orders of life. These differences to modern reptiles, yet shared characteristics across species was, for Owen 'deemed sufficient ground for establishing a distinct tribe or suborder of Saurian Reptiles for which I would propose the name of 'Dinosauria'' (Cadbury 2000, p.249).

He had spent weeks discussing and configuring possible names in the attempt to devise an epithet dramatic enough to distinguish this group of creatures from any living comparisons, and to capture the sense of scale and alterity that these beasts evoked. Owen decided upon a combination of Greek words: *Deinos*, to convey 'terrible', and *sauros*, meaning 'lizard'. However, while Owen may take the credit for naming a new category of animal, their revelatory evolution as modern forms was less immediate.

Owen's classification followed from the work of Georges

Cuvier, a prominent naturalist and geologist who in the late 18th and early 19th centuries did much to facilitate the discourse of palaeontology through his study of geological strata. He was also an early proponent of the theory that species now extinct could have existed in an earlier historical period which was a remarkable opposition to a culture that still had some grounding in the mythic structures of biblical Genesis. Cuvier became the leading authority in a scientific method known as 'comparative anatomy' which compared the bone structures of living animals with those of fossil remains in order to determine the appearance of the living form of the fossilised remains. This comparative method is itself comparable in some way to the study of a cultural fossil, except that this is reversed, attempting to describe the form of the present itself through the remains of extinct forms of its past. Yet, as the recreated creatures show, they are as much a representation of the temporally specific culture of their context as any other form of production or representation.

Owen's act of naming is a formative moment in a process of creation. It is a process that is both ongoing and continually subject to contestation. The dinosaur is a mediated form, arranged according to fragmentary traces. The interpretation of these traces is determined by each present moment of its constitution. The animals themselves have left only the most fragmentary of traces experienced through a complex process of scientific and artistic production. They exist in part through the interpretation and representation of fossil remains and the increasingly sophisticated fields of palaeontology. Of equal significance is the movement of these images and representations through culture. The invention of the dinosaur is consistent with Baudrillard's model of the industrial, or 'second-order' simulacrum (1993, p.55). Baudrillard describes a generation of objects and signs that emerge from the formation of industrial modernity. These are counterfeits from the outset.

They are signs without fixed tradition. Any relationship between original and counterfeit is abolished. Instead of analogy or reflection, the relationships available in the material and semiotic realms are of equivalence and indifference. Within the serial frameworks of the second-order simulacrum, objects become indistinct simulacra of one another. This general law of equivalences is facilitated by the extinction of the original reference.

The first visual image of a dinosaur appeared, long before the term had been applied as a classification, in 1818. It was a drawing by Gideon Mantell who was another key figure in the history of the dinosaur. His drawing was based on fossil teeth and fragmentary samples of bones that he identified as belonging to an extinct reptile, which he later named Iguanadon (meaning 'Iguana tooth'), because the closest link to a contemporary anatomical reference for the teeth was an iguana. This comparative method is a retroactive one, writing prehistory from an understanding of the present, shaping prehistory as an origin. It is the creation of a history of extinct, obsolete forms which were to be replaced by successive orders of animals. The configuration of the extinct object related to the similarities between fragmentary remains and the complete skeleton of a known species. It was illustrative of the fragmented evidence and the process of assembling those pieces. It is sketched as a skeleton in a 'live' pose, suggesting a precedent for the convention of displaying dinosaur skeletons in museums as if they were alive.

However, the defining factor of the drawing is that it represents a literal interpretation of the comparative method. The extinct animal has been imagined as a large version of the comparative model i.e. as an oversized lizard. Mantell's interpretation contains two dominant and visibly obvious errors. The first is the literal interpretation of the Iguanadon as partly crocodilian, partly like a large herd mammal. The second is the placing of an unidentifiable pointed bone. This was interpreted as a rhinoceros-like horn that protruded from the end of the animal's nose. There has since been a shifting of opinion as to whether the animal was bipedal or walked on all fours. Certainly, the four-limbs resemble something more like arms, and are shorter than the hind legs. The shape of the Iguanadon has since been identified as predominantly bipedal, bearing little recognisable resemblance to Mantell's version. The 'horn' has also been identified as a bony spiked 'thumb' protruding from each hand. This defining, original visualisation of a dinosaur was inherently flawed. However, although these flaws ensured a level of inaccuracy that would render this manifestation of the Iguanadon obsolete the comparative method allowed for the conceptualisation of prehistory. This was the recovery of an invisible history.

Mantell's work, and his commitment to recovering an unimaginably distant past, must be recognised as extraordinary. However, in his lifetime, his achievements were usurped by the ruthlessness of Owen - a story told brilliantly by Deborah Cadbury's *The Dinosaur Hunters* (2000). Owen's act of naming was well judged, and paid off. In November 1842, he received the favour of the Crown, and was granted an annual pension from the Civil List. Owen also sought the unification of all collections of natural history into a national collection, and a unified theory of religion and natural order. He pursued these things at the cost of all who might obscure his view to his goals. Both were achieved, to some extent, in what is now known as the Natural History Museum in South Kensington.

Owen's position on evolution shifted somewhat, but the essential force behind his championing the prehistoric can be read as the invention of the dinosaur as a means of emphasising the fact that these fossilised skeletons were distinguishable from any other animal ever known. They were distinct, unrelated to living animals, and thus must represent an earlier order wiped off the planet by God. This emphasis would, for him, have reinforced his opposition to the principle of evolution as ultimately given formal resolution by Darwin. Although Darwin would not publish his *On the Origin of Species* until 1859, despite having formulated the ideas many years previously, arguments for and against concepts of evolution within natural history had been developing through the early nineteenth century. Owen's opposition to evolutionary theories can be seen in the decorative animals that populate the façade of the natural history museum in South Kensington. The apparently random mixture of contemporary, prehistoric and mythic creatures is a deliberately provocative attempt to disavow any notion of an evolutionary progress of animals. For Owen, the invention of the dinosaur reveals a class of reptiles that appear higher than lizards and crocodiles but which are extinct, therefore seemingly undermining a simplistic reading of evolution. This opposition appears absurd today as coming from the man who invented the dinosaur, which is a subject that is particularly evocative of concepts of temporal and biological evolution. Yet Owen's interpretation of the dinosaur was as a dead end- a line that did not progress as an example to dismiss the notion of a changing temporality. He favoured a continuous but staggered theory of creation, in which God introduced successive species in different eras, then wiped them out, or allowed them to die. Since the notion of a great flood had been dismissed by recent geological advances as the cause of their extinction, he speculated that changes in carbon dioxide levels in the air were to blame – a rationale that, although flawed, could have had some appeal in a polluted industrial city such as Victorian London.

This ur-epoch of the prehistoric became a space for ideological representation even as it took shape. The age of the dinosaurs came to be looked upon as an ancient, violent empire that lasted 150 million years. Yet this is an image that was shaped and did not arise immediately. Early attempts to visualise extinct creatures were coloured by the tradition of biblical illustration and depictions of the Garden of Eden. An illustration for the frontispiece of George Richardson's *Sketches in Prose and Verse*, published in 1838, paid homage to Mantell's growing collection of prehistoric creatures. It depicted a pastoral view of an almost happy looking Iguanadon basking on a beach surrounded by other prehistoric creatures. This reinforced Owen's view of prehistoric life as something that was sanctioned and then destroyed by divine force. The influence of the Garden of Eden is one that remained throughout the development and expansion of images of dinosaurs and prehistory in the nineteenth century but I would suggest that the emphasis changed from a static, peaceful and harmonious scene to one of violence, conflict and competition.

In 1838 Mantell commissioned John Martin to produce *Country of the Iguanadon* as a frontispiece for his own book *Wonders of Geology*. The image of creatures fighting, apparently to the death, disrupted the pastoral image with one of savage competition and fuelled the popular idea of a struggle for existence. This idea was proposed in Thomas Malthus's *Essay on Population* of 1798, which drew attention to the danger of population growth outstripping food supplies. This is an essay that was instrumental in Darwin's formulation of the theory that favourable variations within animals would afford them a greater chance of survival than competing animals with less favourable variations. Both within and surrounding the invention of the dinosaur, a new paradigm of political economy and biological knowledge was being defined in terms of competition.

The origins of the decision to have a display of dinosaurs and other recently discovered/invented prehistoric creatures are somewhat hazy, but one thing that is clear is that it was Mantell who was first approached to oversee the project. He declined due to his extremely poor health, and subsequently died soon after in November 1852. Unsurprisingly Owen took hold of the opportunity left by Mantell's reluctant refusal. It seems clear that Paxton was enthusiastic about an idea that fused entertaining spectacle with an informative, educational role, and that Albert was behind the endeavour. Benjamin Waterhouse Hawkins was commissioned in September 1852 by the Crystal Palace Company to build a series of prehistoric animal sculptures and was appointed Director of the Fossil Department of the Crystal Palace. He was a specialised natural history artist who had achieved considerable success and had shown work in the Great Exhibition. The creation of the dinosaurs was to be undertaken under the guidance of Owen. It is the influence of Owen that ensures more errors than were necessary at the time, particularly the shape and aspect of both Iguanadon and Megalosaurus.

The reconstructions were organised around a display not only of dinosaurs but also of marine reptiles and pterosaurs, prehistoric mammals and amphibians, laid out on three islands. Each representing a different geological period, the islands were designed as arrangements of exaggerated geology. This topography narrates an unambiguous and linear account - an archipelago as model of evolutionary sequence. An unrealised aspect of the design was the creation of an artificial tide that could hide and reveal parts of the scene and its inhabitants as the waters rose and fell.

The design of the models involved painstaking research and a high level of accuracy based on existing knowledge. The subjects were chosen as they were each represented by a large number of fossil clues, although none were complete. The bones were drawn in their actual scale, which provided the scale and shape of an outline drawing, which was ultimately defined by comparisons with living animals. This method, while ultimately constructing a scene of historicism and extinction, was used by Owen as an anti-evolutionary argument as it is dependent on archetypal characteristics within all forms of creation. He argued that if progressive evolution were true it would be visible in the history of fossil reptiles as reptiles as a class were considered to be the least fixed in their characteristics and the most transitional in their range of variations. Dinosaurs were the height of an achievement, of which contemporary reptiles were a lower order. Yet he was instrumental in creating a visible record of the evolutionary shape of the discourse which he invented, and for ultimately writing the evolutionary subtext which lurks beneath the narrative of the ruins of the Crystal Palace.

From the drawings made by Hawkins and overseen by Owen a small model was made which was rigorously compared with the understood configurations of the fossils. This would then be reproduced and enlarged to make a copy in clay. Scale was not exaggerated as such, but rather than work to the scale of the most complete specimen the largest fragment of bone would be used as the means to determine the size extrapolating the complete proportions through comparisons with the most complete examples. The full sized animal model would be reworked through comparisons with as wide a range of fossil examples as possible. A mould was then made of the clay figure, which was destroyed in the process. From the mould could be made the final cast. However, these are not cast in a conventional manner. The materials from which they are built would suggest that they were a Victorian architectural structure rather than a sculpture - an officially recognised status as the sculptures are classified as listed buildings. Hawkins lists the materials of the Iguanadon as:

4 iron columns 9 feet long by seven inches diameter, 600 bricks, 650 5-inch half-round drain tiles, 900 plain, 38 casks of cement, 90 casks of broken stone, making a total of 640 bushels of artificial stone. These, with 100 feet of iron hooping and 20 feet of cube inch bar, constitute the bones, sinews and muscles of this large model, the largest of which there is any record of a casting being made. (McCarthy and Gilbert 1994, p.17)

This heavy, industrial materiality is in sharp contrast to the contemporary manifestation of the dinosaur, digitally articulated as a bio-cybernetic, elegant and intelligent creature that moves with a supreme fluidity throughout many levels of culture. No longer is the dinosaur the heavy architectural form. It has evolved into a creature of the cinema and television, the museum, and the natural history documentary. Its components are strings of code – both binary and DNA – rather than concrete and metal.

The industrially architectural quality of the Crystal Palace dinosaurs is further demonstrated by the famous New Year's Eve dinner of 1853 that took place inside the mould of the Iguanadon sculpture, which was supposedly able to accommodate 21 people. In an account taken from Hawkins' own scrapbook, he describes it as having 'the appearance of a wide open Boat with an enclosed arch seven feet high at both ends' (McCarthy and Gilbert 1994, p.93). It is likely that the event was not a flash of originality, but rather that Hawkins borrowed the idea from American painter, collector and naturalist Charles Willson Peale. Owen seized upon it as a publicity stunt to further aggrandize himself. He sat in the space of the head. Opposite him sat Francis Fuller, the Managing Director of the Crystal Palace. Between them, various friends, colleagues and dignitaries, seated within the shell of the dinosaur, the beast submissively restrained, eviscerated, a comedy prop, nothing more than the vessel for self seeking diners.

The dinner, and its widely published image, cements the period of the dinosaurs' construction and presentation as very much Owen's moment, a triumph he was able to appreciate before becoming embroiled in conflicts around the theories of evolution. His ongoing conflict with T.H. Huxley would do much to discredit Owen's position and legacy. Nowhere is this discredited status more visible, ironically, than on the facade of Owen's lasting triumphant legacy in South Kensington, amongst the prehistoric creatures and beasts of myth that share the facade of the Natural History Museum. Today it is so blatant as to not be visible, like the object of Poe's tale *The Purloined Letter*, hidden in plain sight.

The monsters, despite their size and beastly appearance, were diminished by their setting. They retain this sense of domestication today, as harmless and decorative, as well as quaintly archaic. For a Victorian audience, they could adopt a fearsome aspect yet were unthreatening, experienced in safety, and consumed as leisure. The fourteen different prehistoric animals were revealed to an audience as star exhibits, unveiled from the limited sphere of a narrow, predominantly scientific community, as a mass spectacle on an unprecedented scale. They were a publicity sensation, and, as the Crystal Palace charged an entrance fee, a commercial one too. The vast crowds that visited the Crystal Palace, as well as the enormous amount of publicity generated, ensured the proliferation of the dinosaur as a popular image. Yet these popular images have been made obsolete, the knowledge and imagery surrounding prehistoric life is continually updated at an impossibly accelerated pace, from clumsy, industrial monsters to sleek and birdlike computer-generated animals. From its earliest inception, through to its public unveiling in 1854 and right up to the present moment, the dinosaur has been a cultural form that has rendered impossible the precise separation of its science – of palaeontology – from its visualisation.

They are now charmingly harmless and obsolete. The evocation of a bestiary, one whose inhabitants are tame and commodified, overshadowed by the towering fountains and the Palace itself looming above them, has been replaced with something more domestic. The creatures now seem to be an extension of the adjacent city farm, popular with local residents and schools, on the edge of the park. They are endearing, perhaps even a little pathetic, in appearance. They look less like fearful unimaginable ancient beasts than they do bizarre equivalents of the neighbouring pigs and alpacas. Walking downhill, for only a very short distance from the farm, a remarkable vista is revealed, a miniaturised geological diorama. The scaling down brings space and time into an observable whole. The closest part of a tiny archipelago is the earliest point in a temporal excursion. We are at the most distant point in time. From here on in we are on a brief stroll into the age of recent, the post-deluvian.

By the water's edge are footprints cast in concrete and these are all that is left of a longer trail from the 1850s. These are indexical traces of tracks, found in sandstone across England, of some squat, chubby beasts. There are three of them here, one smooth creature, flanked by scaly relatives. Each rests upon concrete circles. The backs arch into humps, legs tucked in beneath them. These are Labyrinthodons. The name might elicit something far more bestial. Or perhaps evoke a nobler form of beast, a grander, more imperious, fearsome Minotaur. A few minutes walk away is a true labyrinth, recently redesigned by the Girl Guides, comprised of living hedge walls, with a stone map of itself at its centre. Alas, these gentle looking monsters need no such elaborate prisons. The name derives from the group designation Labyrinthodontia, as the interior of their teeth. When studied in cross section these teeth reveal curving patterns resembling maze-like paths. The species name reveals more about the process of discovery, identification, and classification that precede reconstruction, than it does the creature itself. This is a process of working with fragments, focusing on details, on fossilised bones, teeth, claws. The minutiae of splintered remnants identified the group before any manifested speculation of an animal's appearance.

Two varieties of Labyrithodon squat upon the tiny beaches of the island. One is the Labyrinthodon Salamandroides, the other Labyrinthodon Pachygnathus, the latter part of the names taking in a broader visual morphology, describing the smooth skinned variety as akin to a salamander, and the thickjaw of the other. Amazingly, these frog monsters are ancestors of us all. Or rather to all vertebrates that live on the land. Alongside the group are some other creatures with a familiar, turtle-like aspect. Like the Labyrinthodons, Dicynodon was named after its teeth, visibly protruding from the upper jaw. Already looking more cuddly than fierce, this name, meaning 'two dog teeth', suggests domestication. Yet there is no evidence to support the animals' wearing of shells on their backs. These are not just an error of interpretation, but are in all likelihood a pure invention, or, at least an interpolation. However, the nature of such errors is not unique to these creatures, or to the Crystal Palace, but demonstrates both the need to fill in gaps in what can be deduced from available fossil evidence, but also to find legible points of reference for an audience to read. In this case, legibility is provided though likening the creature to a turtle. Such interpolation is still common today, most visibly with the colouring of dinosaurs. Colour is required for the purposes of representation, but of course there is no evidence as to this aspect of appearance.

The meeting of land and water is emphatically central to the display. Labyrinthodon and Dicynodon both seem to have dragged themselves up onto land, counterintuitively to Owen's antievolutionary position, yet suggestive of a liminal and unsettling quality of these animals, at home in either space. The strangest such breaching of the surface is an Icthyosaur basking among the wild flowers and long grasses. It rears its cold grey head, a gazing eye looking already fossilised. Only the teeth seem to offer something animated. The Icthyosaur is beached deliberately in accordance with Owen's belief that Icthyosaurs were able to crawl out of the water like a seal. This interpretation was based on observing the bones that connect the fore-fins to the body. The structure of the fin is distinct, according to Owen, from dolphins, whereas marine animals that leave the water have it. This seems like a fairly reasonable comparative deduction, but has since been dismissed - Icthyosaurs are now considered to be completely aquatic.

Other mistakes are morphological, and not drastic. These specimens lack the shark-like dorsal fins and tails revealed by later fossil discoveries. Instead the tail of the Icthyosaurus Communis, wallowing on a slab of concrete by the water's edge, is like a crumpled paddle. The other, more visually striking, feature that is incorrect is the extraordinary skeletal eye. Segmented with bony plates it looks like an already fossilised part of a living animal. The bones are called sclerotic plates, and were possibly used in adjusting focal length. These plates would have been, it is now considered, below the external surfaces of the eye, and would not have been visible. The material remains have dictated the appearance of the representation in too great a degree. They are over-visible.

There are two species of Icthyosaurs on show, and their origin is connected to the central narrative thread of fossil discovery and the formation of a modern understanding of prehistoric life as the traces of their remains were initially gathered by the Anning family. Mary Anning, and her brother Joseph, can take the credit for finding the first complete and articulated Icthyosaur skeleton to which the Crystal Palace versions owe their general form. It was the skull that was discovered first and it was originally mistaken for a crocodile's due to its reptilian appearance. Anning's life, perhaps not untypically for the early nineteenth century, reads as hard surrounded as it was by misfortune and a high rate of mortality. Her biography now fuels the heritage and tourist culture of twenty first-century Lyme Regis, but her place within the history of geology and palaeontology is well deserved. Working class, self educated, marginalised by sex, discriminated by religious difference, she had a thoroughness of approach to the collecting of fossils that was to contribute to the transformation of modernity. Yet discriminatory boundaries were to isolate her from the mainstream of scientific institutions and deny her recognition.

Anning was uncovering traces of life from the Mesozoic oceans embedded in cliffs and scattered across beaches. These remnants must have been a source of a most extreme kind of cognitive estrangement. There may have been centuries of speculation regarding how natural processes reshaped the surface of the Earth, but the more recent era of Christian dogma, of biblical temporality, of a world determined by the narratives of scripture, must have ossified the sense of the present. This was conflated with the sense of an ordered history of mankind, one of progress, resulting in the present. This scale of time was conceivable in terms of thousands of years, a time only as old as the humans who measure it. Around the beached Icthyosaurs are three Plesiosaurs, another species associated with Anning's finds at Lyme. They have emerged from the water. For the purposes of conservation, they, like all the aquatic creatures, are kept raised above water on their concrete bases. Or, rather, the water is kept low, away from contact with the monsters, and as a result, fails to divide the islands as intended.

If the fossilised remains Anning and others uncovered were often initially attributed as the remains of crocodiles, it is apt, but also disorientating; to find them sharing the display at the Crystal Palace with these with these newly invented extinct creatures. These two ancestors of modern crocodiles are Teleosaurs, long snouted, like gavials, salt water reptiles whose physiology suggests a life led more in water than on land. They appear familiar, and closer to an impression of life-like realism than their neighbours. As ancestors to living animals, the Teleosaurs may look slightly unusual with their extended snouts, but they look convincing, and do not lag behind contemporary impressions of such a species. Yet not only do they resemble crocodiles, forging an uncanny connection with our own era, but their name itself forges, albeit unintentionally, a sense of particular temporality at work in the intentional configuration of the Crystal Palace - a forceful demonstration of natural and cultural historical forces as teleological. All of the past orientated towards the present.

The islands may no longer be separated - there was never much distance between them anyway - but there is a significant shift that occurs with the next two sets of animals. Trees and foliage have forged a new landscape dividing these enormous monsters from their neighbours. The impression is that they are on another land mass, albeit at a level of miniaturisation. Following the circuitous path along the water's edge plays out as a proto-theme park ride through time. Scale is re-orientated. These things are bigger than us and exceed the measure of domesticity. Two great beasts seem to move away from the earliest scene, their backs to the Icthyosaurs and Plesiosaurs, slowly plodding towards obsolescence.

Megalosaurus demonstrates an imposing size, a materiality that is solid, and a posture that is convincing. The surface texture is worked in bold rather than fine detail, perfect for the scale of the creature. The detail of the thick, wrinkled folds around the eye gives Megalosaurus an animalistic verisimilitude, and something approaching the appearance of a personality. Such details of facture, and our closeness to them in a line of sight, bring to mind the distinctions between the immaterial excesses of computer generated imagery in the mainstream cinema of the fantastic, and the contrast with the detailed renderings exemplified Willis O'Brien and Ray Harryhausen, who created animated monsters that dazzled audiences with unsettling movement, facture and illusion. These latter two elements really come into play here.

Megalosaurus plods along behind the spiky Hylaeosaurus. The pair seem to be acting out herd behaviour, but considering the carnivorous nature of the Megalosaur, it would be more accurate to think of this is a predatory stalk. If so, it is an empty gesture amongst the static, edenic calm presented here. The struggle for survival of selection that was to dominate after the publication in 1859 of Darwin's *Origin* had yet to surface. For Owen, the foundational determinants of nature were laws set by God. These creatures were created and destroyed by no other force. Facing off against these two giants are Iguanadons. Their overall form here determined by Owen against Mantell's assertion that their forelimbs were short suggesting that they might be predominantly bipedal. The disparity between these representations of Iguanadon and those that followed is due to Owen's particular stubbornness. The same misrepresentation applies to the Megalosaurus, which stood with the more familiar stance of a Tyrannosaurus Rex. The four behemoths on this island are less like lizards, but take as their model giant herbivorous mammals. They are rhinocerotic. Indeed, it is Dürer's illustration of a rhinoceros as an armoured beast from

1515 that seems to serve as an ancestor for the sculptures.

The path continues through beautifully restored constructed indicators of geological time: illusions of rock strata, giant elk, mammals grazing on a distant shore, and a towering sloth clinging desperately to a dead tree. However, despite appearances, these monsters are not obsolete failures. They represent a model of a particular moment, but in doing so remind us that any moment is just that, and will soon be superseded, made obsolete, built upon, moved away from. Received ideas become myths, yet this doesn't take away from the radical edge these objects possessed, and still possess. They represent cutting edge science, epoch defining shifts in knowledge, new perceptions of history, not just of culture but the history of all life. The Crystal Palace monsters embody amazing acts of perception, and interpretation. They preserve ideas that shattered received understandings of the world. They are critical thought made solid in enduring representational forms. It is far more important to realise what is correct here, than to follow the line that they are laughably inaccurate and obsolete. These are treasures of the last century, not embarrassing remains. Despite the hubris of Owen's intentions, these are images of an enormous humility, situating human life in a newly configured relation to the age of earth and the processes of life. This may be domesticated entertainment on display, but is nevertheless a spectacle that carried within it the most chastising of narratives.

Perhaps most importantly, they give shape to historical conflict. They embody the contested and shifting aspects of scientific knowledge. Not only would these preserved forms have been created differently in later decades, but would have been realised differently under Mantell's control. What they offer as evidence is even greater than a simple mistake or misconception in themselves, as is so often assumed. These objects are astonishing. Their status as failures is a miscomprehension reflective of an obsession with the new. This condition in which the mythic new is venerated regards all that is not new as mere style, as flawed, quaint, assimilable. At stake in this miscomprehension is the difference between obsolescence as a critique of fashion or as its effect. They may be fossils, but fossils of extraordinary complexity and sophistication. Their temporal distance is misleading. These objects need to be readdressed as of an equal significance to Darwin's *Origin*.

The sense of an insect trapped in amber that these preserved creatures evoke corresponds to a museological desire for illusion, to a desire to witness a preserved and static object. Yet in Michael Crichton's novel *Jurassic Park*, and Steven Spielberg's cinematic adaptation, the fossil becomes more than animal remains transformed by geological forces into solid rock, offering clues as to the appearance and behaviour. The insect in amber contains the life blood, the magic essence of the dinosaur, that through the methodical application of technology, can resurrect the long extinct. The fantasy brings about equivalence with us as subjects with increasingly realisable fears and fantasies of cloning. Animals can now be cloned, and cloned meat has entered the food chain for human consumption. Claims have been made that human cloning has already taken place. The cultures of modernity assimilate and perpetuate techniques of cloning and duplication as well as technological and systematic replication. Cloning is a process of synthesis, of combination and manipulation. Even restoration takes on the aspect of cloning, of replacing, reproducing, substituting, in combinations. The restored monsters have now been brought more fully within the circuit of representation of prehistory, like the Albert Memorial, remade into ambiguous relics, which only become troubling when looked at closely.

As well as being subject to processes of cloning these charming animals are victims of a catastrophe the likes of which can only exist within the fantastic narratives of science fiction and cinema. This is not a metaphor. The presentation of the extinct has had a century and a half to infiltrate strands of conscious and unconscious modernity. There has been a shift from biblical flood as a cause of extinction to possibilities that test the limits of imagination. Whatever caused the death of so many animals, must have been bigger, more devastating, than mere inundation. Of course, cataclysm was less prevalent than evolution. Cataclysm is something that has grown around the dinosaur like the changing foliage of their islands. An evolutionary struggle has slowly reached a point of realisation that the ultimate fate of this lost world was in all likelihood due to a celestial body of some form, an asteroid or a comet, striking the Yucatan Peninsula.

This destroyer from space was, it is believed, 6 miles across, the impact ejecting enough rock to form a crater that at its widest is 175 miles in diameter. It is an event that is hard to picture - perhaps an irony considering the fascination with both popular cinema and science fiction narratives for catastrophes. Cinematic representations have translated catastrophic tropes by an evolving process of technological representation, into a norm, accompanied by the brief shocking moment of 11th September 2001, when it seemed, as Baudrillard pointed out, that we were watching a realisation of fantasies played out many times before (2002). The explosion would have released energy at a scale that would be two million time more powerful than the most destructive of nuclear weapons, the equivalent of one hundred million megatons. Ash and steam would have been sent out from the explosion eradicating everything in its way. Rock from the excavated ground, and from the rock itself, would have been sent at speeds to actually leave Earth's atmosphere, to re-enter as fiery meteors to further scorch the surface of the planet, setting huge swathes of it alight.

The collision would have inevitably caused tsunamis that would have reached heights of thousands of feet. The dinosaurs were propelled forward, like Benjamin's Angel of History, then to be swept up by the force of another explosion - The Great Exhibition. The spread of the influence of this event was global, but the ruins of the Crystal Palace offer a site of intensified evidence, part of a crater that spreads about 40 miles or so from the epicentre in South Kensington.

Chapter 3

Use and Enchantment

Across the lawn in front of the Oxford Museum of Natural History a set of footprints cross in a diagonal trail. Overlooking them is the gothic revival facade of William Butterfield's Keble College. The brick surfaces are partitioned by sharp symmetrical patterns, visual metaphors for primeval construction, depicting geological strata of the Earth's surface as decorative intersections of the building's exterior. The footprints belong to Megalosaurus, the rhinocerotic carnivore that hunts on the Crystal Palace islands, where his prints once formed a trail for promenading visitors of Sydenham to follow, now lost, save for a solitary concrete trace.

Inside, the proto-modernist grid of the Crystal Palace has grown into a soaring organic, ornate gothic tracery of glass and iron. The impression is in part of something like an incandescent cathedral, but these might also be the bare limbs of trees silhouetted against a bright, even sky. This metal framework also resembles the structures of plants that had made such an impression on Joseph Paxton, suggesting the ability of a thin frame to support an entire building, while the arched ceiling girders are like the ribs of a mighty cetacean. Daylight floods in through the glass roof, providing the museum interior with uncommonly vivid illumination. The sharply contrasted tones of metal and sky find other points of resemblance in the two dinosaur skeletons in the centre of the space. The first to greet visitors is Iguanadon. It stands tall, in a fully upright pose. Forelimbs held in front of it as short arms, pointed thumbs up in their permanently comical gesture as if to indicate that palaeontology got things right this time, having taken this piece off its nose. However, the recognisable pose is not entirely up to date. A caption tactfully points out that Iguanadon probably did spend time upright, but that the forelimbs were also likely to be used as legs. A colour illustration shows it on all fours, bringing us back to the Owen's quadrupedal beasts, albeit in a more streamlined form.

Behind it rears a skeleton of the most famous of real monsters, Tyrannosaurus Rex, an icon of the Cretaceous period, eclipsing the dwindled fame of Megalosaurus. A life-sized model of the head of a T Rex can be found nearby. It is placed low down, so as to look into the eyes of its audience, and tempt younger visitors to put their heads between its teeth. Yet the best indicator of the distance travelled between here and Sydenham comes in the form a beautifully colourful Utah Raptor, its orange back and dark blue markings striking a remarkable affinity with the decorative brickwork that adorns the museum's interior. The fearsome Raptor faces a row of display cases that frame dinosaurs in the broader narrative of their nineteenth century origins. As the basis for the Velociraptors of *Jurassic Park*, this is not some preposterous giant, but is scaled to our own frames. It is the inverse of the Crystal Palace monsters: bird-like, bipedal, intelligent, fast and unambiguously viscous.

However, at the back of the well lit, open and vaulted space of the Oxford Museum of Natural History, past the neatly arranged cases and displays, a small doorway takes us into another world, into another distinct manifestation of the 1851 catastrophe. We step through into a brief moment of minimalist illumination, a white, artificially-lit platform floating in the dark, with small gift shop on one side, and information area on the other. Beyond the glare, the platform provides us with a view into the gloom of the ground floor of the Pitt Rivers Museum.

Having passed through from the bright world of enlightenment and nature's order visitors descend a set of steps into a netherworld. This is a world that is darker- both metaphorically and visually. It seems chaotic, filled with the tenebrocity of Victorian England's Other. Faced with the dizzyingly intense accumulation of objects, and the wooden display cases, there is an illusion of temporal displacement. The received impossibility of our having travelled backwards in time is counterbalanced by an assuring presupposition that the museum has been preserved as the example of another age, like the historical courts of the Crystal Palace in Sydenham. You could be forgiven for imagining that this spectacle was a fossil from a previous epoch, flawlessly preserved like an insect trapped in amber. The overall appearance and stubbornly anachronistic character of the interior tends to support this image. Dominated by a huge totem pole at one end and a suspended outrigger canoe at the other, the museum is filled with nineteenth-century-style vitrines, tightly packed with barely enough room to move between them. Raised above this scene are two narrow balcony floors tracing the edges of the interior space, supported by iron columns that reach up to form arched ceiling supports. Yet this overall impression, while dramatic and full of evocative character and charm, is not in itself what is so peculiarly resonant about the museum.

Inside the cases a seemingly innumerable number of things have been put on display, their quantity and diversity appearing overwhelming, limitless and even chaotic. While some of the labels have a contemporary feel and have been printed, many are aged and have been written in tiny but immaculate handwriting, bearing indexical traces of presumably long-lost hand at work in the cataloguing and interpreting of this material. Many of the cases rest atop chests of drawers, unlocked to visitors, revealing intimate encounters with material that exists in limbo between display and storage. Throughout the museum, objects that appear both fascinatingly exotic, yet often strangely familiar, are grouped together in a manner that itself represents an unfamiliar system of thought.

The only things not here are objects of mass production. In comparison to the contemplative order that museums generally seem to present, the abundance of artefacts appears excessive, the arrangements lacking proper separation, instead giving way to overcrowding, things spilling over, seeming to clash and overlap.

Clustered together by commonalities of type of form, of use, familial groups of artefacts can be found in vitrines that appear to constitute individual departments. Classificatory headings announce Snuff Taking Appliances, Ball Games and Methods of Making Fire. A collection of flutes and whistles includes pieces shaped as people and animals that were sold as tourist souvenirs in Mallorca and collected in the 1950s. Amongst hand crafted water vessels, an ostrich egg used by a Kalahari Bushman takes pride of place. A case filled with religious deities can be found in propinquity to a series of shrunken heads, stringed instruments, votive offerings, and a witch in a bottle from a village near Hove. Looking at these objects, reading the variety of labels, it becomes clear that this is not a piece of the nineteenth century trapped in amber. This is a growing collection committed to the unlimited richness of the everyday, whether that is one that is familiar to visitors or characterized by an undeniable feeling of alterity. Yet this sense of alterity is not straightforward. The range of ages of collection here span between colonial and post colonial eras. The Other is not that as imagined by a fixed point in the past, but rather there are traces of the growth and transformation of Otherness through anthropology's disciplinary growth and transformation, with a focus upon the everyday. A sense of the importance of the everyday is illuminated, not as mundane and separate from other aspects of culture, but as its fabric, hinting at the centrality of objects in relation to models of selfhood and identity. Yet this is not some chaotic *wunderkammer* or an unsystematic fleamarket lacking an imposed framework of order. Rather it is a different system of order, one that is unfamiliar but which is no less systematic than that of any other museum, perhaps more so than many.

The museum's founder was Lieutenant-General Augustus Henry Lane Fox Pitt Rivers (1827 - 1900). He only took the name Pitt Rivers upon succeeding the title and property of the sixth Lord Rivers in 1880 (To avoid confusion, I will refer to him consistently as Pitt Rivers, although many sources refer to him as Lane Fox if addressing a point in history before 1880). He entered the Royal Military Academy at Sandhurst in 1841 and was commissioned into the Grenadier Guards in 1845. Early in his military career, he was given the task of investigating methods that could potentially improve the type of rifle used in the British Army, its use and the methods of instruction employed. In seeking to determine qualities of improvement in weaponry, he speculated that this was effected by means gradual changes. Asserting the regularity of this process, he believed it to be a universal rule of evolution that applied to other ideas and objects and it was in order to test and illustrate these views that he began, in 1851, to collect systematically. This date is not a coincidence or minor detail. It is clear that the Great Exhibition that made concrete a desire to collect, and demonstrated the potential for public and instructive sequences of display (Bowden 1991, p.47).

His system of classification comprised of groups into which objects of like form or function were associated to form a series.He introduced the term typology to describe his method. Within these main groups objects belonging to the same region could then form local sub-groups. Where objects could be utilized to do so, they would be arranged so as to suggest a sequence that suggested the possible evolution of the particular class. This type of arrangement was particularly applied to objects from the same region, as this was thought to be more illustrative of a sequential continuity. This sequence was envisioned as one that moved from the most primitive to the most complex and specialized, the primitive end of the scale in closest proximity to natural forms. He allegorized typology as a tree of progress that distinguishes the leading shoots from the inner branches and believed that this method was itself the evidential key to understanding human culture.

At this time, the anthropological discipline was still in an embryonic state. Social phenomena had been identified as a subject of study by Saint-Simon in France, and the subject of sociology had been named by Auguste Comte, whose laws of social life were based on the assumption that all societies evolved through the same stages and that a drive towards improvement was a fundamental principle, a belief that, as Balfour makes clear, was recognized in Pit Rivers' system:

> It was a fundamental principle of Colonel Lane Fox that in the arts and customs of the still living savage and barbaric peoples there are reflected to a considerable extent the various strata of human culture in the past, and that it is possible to reconstruct in some degree the life and industries of Man in prehistoric times by a study of existing races in corresponding stages of civilization. (Myers 1906, p.XIV)

Nineteenth-century thought in this area was characterized by an evolutionism largely influenced, in Britain, by Herbert Spencer, whose ideas about the survival of the fittest were later attributed to Darwin. Pitt Rivers' notion of evolution, which was solidified by the interpretations that followed the publication of Darwin's *The Origin of Species* in 1859, is a model that privileges his present moment of Western civilization as the inevitable conclusion of successive progression, and that sees other cultures as different stages of primitive, inferior form. The system is described by Balfour:

> The Earth, as we know, is peopled with races of the most

heterogeneous description, races in all stages of culture. Colonel Lane Fox argued that, making due allowance for possible instances of degradation from a higher condition, this heterogeneity could readily be explained by assuming that, while the progress of some races has received relatively little check, the cultural development of other races has been retarded to a greater or less extent, and that we may see represented conditions of at least partially arrested development. In other words, he considered that in the various manifestations of culture among the less civilized peoples were to be seen more or less direct survivals from the earlier stages or strata of human evolution; vestiges of ancient conditions which have fallen out at different points and have been left behind in the general march of progress.(Myers 1906, pp.XIV-XV)

For Pitt Rivers the central point in his thinking about the development of material culture was analogous to the evolution of natural forms described by Darwin, and his ideas were more focused after reading the book in 1859. However, there was no such convincing analogy there for Darwin, who rejected the idea that the idea of adaptation was bound to the notion of progress (Gould 1987, p.37). There is an apparent scientific, objective quality to evolution, as Darwin attempted to outline, but this is lost in the idea of social evolution.

The collection outgrew his home and from 1874 to 1878 it was exhibited in the newly opened Bethnal Green Museum - today known as the Museum of Childhood. This site was connected to the Great Exhibition through direct lineage. It was a branch of the South Kensington Museum that had been planted deliberately in this predominantly working class area in London's East End, in order, in the eyes of the accumulating institutional forces forged by the Great Exhibition, to affect a positive and instructive influence upon local people. This appealed to Pitt Rivers, as both the pedagogic imperative of the museum and its newness - therefore its flexibility - suited his intentions. The collection remained his property and he had the right to add to or subtract from it at will. Upon the public opening of the display, Pitt Rivers read a paper that outlined his methods for a special meeting held by the Anthropological Institute in the museum, which serves as the definitive source of how the collection was originally intended to be organized and displayed, and which highlights the central role of evolution.

The collection was divided into four parts, the first of which referred to physical anthropology, consisting of skulls and hair. Two and three were described by Pitt Rivers himself as follows:

> The remainder of the collection is devoted to objects illustrating the development of prehistoric and savage culture, and consists of – Part II. The weapons of existing savages. Part III. Miscellaneous arts of modern savages, including pottery and substitutes for pottery; modes of navigation, clothing, textile fabrics, and weaving; personal ornament; realistic art; conventionalized art; ornamentation; tools; household furniture; musical instruments; idols and religious emblems; specimens of the written character of races; horse furniture; money and substitutes for money; firearms; sundry smaller classes of objects, such as mirrors, spoons, combs, games, and a collection of implements of modern savages, arranged to illustrate the mode of hafting stone implements. (Myers 1906, p.1)

The fourth part of the collection was made up of prehistoric material that included material classified as specimens of natural forms that simulated artificial ones and also contained modern forgeries for comparison with genuine prehistoric implements, presumably in order to counter the then roaring trade in fakes.

Pitt Rivers is explicit that the focus of the collection is not on objects that are characterised as unique, or that are surprising through their beauty or value. Instead the aim is towards instruction:

> For this purpose ordinary and typical specimens, rather than rare objects, have been selected and arranged in sequence, so as to trace, as far as practicable, the succession of ideas by which the minds of men in a primitive condition of culture have progressed from the simple to the complex, and from the homogenous to the heterogeneous.' (Myers 1906, p.2)

For Pitt Rivers, this collection performed a function that he found absent in other ethnographic collections, which in his opinion would generally not attempt anything other than a geographical arrangement. He attributes this to sociology's marginal status as a science, in contrast to the acknowledgement of the necessity of complex arrangements in classifying and displaying natural history collections. He also sees a problem in the methods of collecting, as the travellers who provide the material have not yet adapted to systematic methods, hence problematizing any attempts at a scientific arrangement. Travellers acquired ethnological objects, in Pitt Rivers' view, not in terms of variety, affinity, or sequence, or with any regard to history or context, but as curiosities. Yet these objects would be none the less valuable if collected without the influence of interpretative theories and if collected in sufficient number and variety to render classification possible. The arrangement of the collection at Bethnal Green was site-specific to the exhibition space, using the available space to demonstrate the succession of ideas he claimed were identifiable in the artefacts. The display would alter to suit whatever environment it was placed in, but in each instance, the objective would remain the same.

Although emphasizing this primary differentiation of geographical system and the typological method Pitt Rivers was developing, he recognized that there were advantages and disadvantages in both:

> By a geographical or racial arrangement the general culture of each distinct race is made the prominent feature of the collection, and it is therefore more strictly ethnological, whereas in the arrangement which I have adopted, the development of specific ideas and their transmission from one people to another, or from one locality to another, is made more apparent, and it is therefore of greater sociological value. (Myers 1906, p.3)

It is worth looking at the qualitative distinction between these terms. Ethnology can essentially be conceptualized as the comparative and historical study of cultures. Anthropologist Alfred Radcliffe-Brown (1881-1955) later distinguished ethnology, meaning the historical-geographical study of peoples, from the functional study of social systems which he termed social anthropology. Ethnology's comparative and historical study combines historical and field study of the popular, folk and tribal cultures with cross-cultural comparison and general-ization. Sociology, termed by Comte and developed by Emile Durkheim was proposed as a study with social facts as the central concern. Durkheim did not distinguish sociology from anthro-pology, though the distinction was to emerge in British and US social scientific circles as the two disciplines developed and drew upon different theoretical, methodological and empirical sources. The differentiation mobilized here is between a notion of particular, specific, cultures and a general sense of human evolution, in which objects representing particular cultures provide useful illustrations of a totalizing principle. The position of early sociological thought, associated with Comte, was an assumption that all cultures moved along the same fundamental trajectory of improvement, regardless of the historical or geographic particularities of that culture or any other factors, and without questioning the very concept of improvement itself. Although Pitt Rivers recognizes the value of the ethnological approach, he again reinforces his preference for demonstrating an evolutionary perspective. He does however acknowledge an ideal scenario in which museums would demonstrate both ethnological and sociological tendencies.

By 1878 the Bethnal Green Museum was incapable of housing the growing collection and it was transferred to the main branch of the South Kensington Museum. Again, it was still his property and he reserved the right to add to and subtract from it. Yet he was seeking to maintain control over it, attempting to impose his authority over museum staff. Although his property, its status as part of such a public museum meant that the collection was not under his direct control, a situation that led to many disagreements. In 1879 the authorities of the South Kensington Museum demanded that the position be clarified – either the museum be granted complete control over the collection or it would not agree to display it. It was very soon after this that Pitt Rivers inherited the Rivers estates. This vast increase in wealth enabled him to re-conceptualize his collection on a far more ambitious scale. He demanded more room and also hinted that he might make a gift of the collection to the museum. A committee was set up to consider the situation with Pitt Rivers maintaining his insistence that he have control over its display in his lifetime. The committee itself was in favour of this proposal but it was rejected by the Council of Education, who ultimately controlled the museum. In seeking an alternative permanent home for the collection that would allow for both the correct format of display and for subsequent expansion, Pitt Rivers began to think that perhaps a university might be a more appropriate choice, as it would be more suited to his explicitly instructive mode of display. He offered the entire collection to the University of Oxford:

He had a considerable respect for a number of Oxford scientists, especially his friend George Rolleston. It was perhaps Rolleston's early death in 1881 that finally decided him to give his collection to Oxford University as a 'gesture to Rolleston's memory'. (Bowden 1991, p.51)

The conditions of the offer were for a site to house the collection, which would not be used for any other purpose, and for the appointment of a lecturer whose subjects would be those of the collection.

The University accepted the offer and met the conditions, and constructed the site that is still the museum's main building. Edward Burnett Tylor was appointed as the first lecturer in anthropology in Britain. He also had the now obsolete title of Keeper of the University Museum. As there was no ethnological department at the University the collection was put under the overall control of Professor H. N. Moseley, Head of the Department of Zoology and Comparative Anatomy. Henry Balfour was one of the zoology graduates that had helped Moseley in the transferring of the collection to its new home, who continued to work on its arrangement and as an assistant to Tylor. In 1891 Balfour was elected as Curator of the Pitt Rivers Museum. However, this arrangement was not an amicable one. He argued frequently with Tylor and Balfour and from 1884 Pitt Rivers was prevented by Tylor from exercising any control over the collection. In the following years the collection expanded often through the wholesale acquisition or transferal of other collections. This included the ethnographic collections of the Asmolean Museum in Oxford in 1886, which incorporated a number of items from the founding Tradescant collection. Tylor's contributions include a forty-foot totem pole from British Columbia that now stands in the museum. Balfour also contributed much to the expansion of the collection, including material obtained as a result of his own travels, and continued to lecture at the museum throughout his career:

> Characteristic of him was a story he told us during a lecture on bows and arrows, to the effect that on one occasion when he was working alone in the Museum, he pricked himself with a poisoned arrow. It was Sunday, and no one was within reach. He sat down with a pencil and paper ready to describe his symptoms until the end. After about an hour, during which no symptoms appeared, he realised that there was not to be an end, and concluded that the passage of time had deprived the poison of its virulence. He finished the story with a warning to students to take no chances with poisoned arrows, or they might not be so lucky. (Blackwood 1991, p.8)

The organization of the collection was elaborated upon by Balfour's successor, Thomas K. Penniman, who took over from Balfour after his death in 1939. He introduced a card cataloguing system and a uniform system of numbering artefacts. Until this point, the record keeping system had been an accessions register, begun at the inception of the museum. These books listed all artefacts with the name of the collector, donor and/or vendor, together with any associated documentation. The task of transcribing the accessions books in duplicate onto Regional and Subject index cards was accomplished during World War II. The cards were recorded on microfilm and subsequently on microfiche and since 1986 all new accessions have been entered in a computer databasewith the gradual addition of the rest of the collection. In addition to initiating the development of the museum's organizational systems, Penniman also established a photographic studio and laboratories for the conservation and restoration of specimens. He also continued to modify the collections in a way that differed from the strict order laid out by Pitt Rivers himself. However, where the system was adhered to, it was conceptualized in a radically different way, reflecting the changing sensibilities of anthropological thought:

> The arrangement of large collections by subjects, with the
> areas in which objects are found as sub-groups within them,
> the original idea of General Pitt Rivers, sometimes displays
> the geographical variation of an art or industry, or the
> diffusion of an art or technique over a wide area, or the origin
> and development of an instrument, process, art or industry,
> and on occasion may simply set out a complete technical
> process, art or industry, and on occasion may simply set out
> a complete technical process in the areas in which it is found,
> or, again, show a classification of all the forms which a
> particular kind of instrument or object may take. (Blackwood
> 1991, p.16)

In this statement by Penniman from the 1950s, the idea of a broad
representation of the variations of a particular form has replaced
the idea of an evolutionary system of progression. There is no
sense of Pitt Rivers' stated intention of demonstrating a specific
form of progress and instead the material has been freely reinter-
preted.

The card index system is contained in 473 file drawers, and
was arranged principally by Beatrice Blackwood who worked
for the museum for forty eight years until her death in 1976. It is
a key element in the process of reinterpretation, offering an
alternative overview to the collection, other than that dictated by
Pitt Rivers himself. The classificatory process itself is a
generative device, one that Blackwood had to invent in order to
manage the collection. Her system was later published as *The
Classification of Artefacts in the Pitt Rivers Museum, Oxford*
(Blackwood 1970) in which she maintains, like Penniman, that
the systems is essentially that of Pitt Rivers 'with some
modifications dictated by experience and the growth of the
collections' (Blackwood 1991, p.15). Yet this seems to gloss over

the difference, that Pitt Rivers was concerned first and foremost with demonstrating a general principle of evolutionary improvement across all human culture and history, from the primitive to the civilized. Even the scope of the museum's investigation appears to have changed: 'The museum takes the world for its province, and for its period, from the earliest times to the present day, excluding the results of mass production' (Blackwood 1991, p.16). Yet it is not the reach of the museum's collecting net that has altered, but in effect the terms in which it is described and conceptualized.

The classificatory system is, in simplified terms, a list of alphabetically arranged groups that are then sub-divided. The following passage is an example page of the version published in 1970:

TOOLS OTHER THAN UNHAFTED IMPLEMENTS (cont.)

Unclassified tools
Wheelwrights' tools
Wood-workers' tools

TORTURE AND PUNISHMENT

For self-torture as a ritual act, see under RELIGION
Fetters
    Stocks
Man-traps
    Catch poles
Poisons for trial by ordeal
Whips

TOYS AND GAMES

Animal toys

Babies' toys
Backgammon
Ball games
    Balls for general purposes
    Carved balls
    Bowls
    Cricket
    Croquet
    Cup-and-ball
    Fives
    Football
    Hockey
    Lacrosse
    Lawn tennis
    Pelota
    Polo
    Rackets (for unspecified games)
    Shinny
    Stool-ball
    Battle-dove and shuttlecock
Board games not otherwise classified
Card games not otherwise classified
Card games
Chess

This system could be interpreted as an adaptive reworking of Pitt Rivers' ideas, a typological methodology, but what is absent from this layout is precisely that which Pitt Rivers wished to display. The nineteenth-century evolutionary model is replaced by that which appears, by contemporary standards, to be a more rational, pragmatic and somewhat more objective schema, in which it is the act of classification itself that occupies the museum's centre. By focusing on the classificatory system as Pitt Rivers' legacy, the museum has been able to find a constructive means with which to address some of the problematic nineteenth-century attitudes that it inherited.

However, it is, of course, the mode of display – which incorporates modes of classification in its arrangement – that provides the primary form of encounter for visitors. Pitt Rivers' typographic system was dependent on very specific modes of display in order to best demonstrate his theories of evolutionary progress. Therefore the developing museum, which has had to incorporate the continual process of reinterpreting its founder's intentions, has also had to reinterpret its mode of display. An obvious problem lies in the history behind the close proximity of archaeological and ethnological material. It is clear that for Pitt Rivers, objects defined by these two disciplines possessed a degree of inter-changeability:

> Following the orthodox scientific principle of reasoning from the known to the unknown, I have commenced my descriptive catalogue with the specimens of the arts of existing savages, and have employed them, as far as possible, to illustrate the relics of primaeval men, none of which, except those constructed of the more imperishable materials, such as flint and stone, have survived to our time. All the implements of primaeval man that were of decomposable materials have disappeared, and can be replaced only in imagination by studying those of his neatest congener, the modern savage. (Myers 1906, p.4)

In this schema, ethnological artefacts can stand in as substitutes for objects from the distant past that have not survived. The so-called primitive societies are literally representative of prehistoric stages of humanity's development, and objects from these societies can be fitted comfortably among objects from geographically and historically distant locations.

One example of how the evolutionist implications of this

method have been softened has been to acknowledge the importance of bringing ethnology and archaeology together, so that the one may be informed and illuminated by the other: 'This precept, that Ethnology and Archaeology are the present and the past of the same subject, man as he was and as he is', has always been a guiding principle in the functioning of the Pitt Rivers Museum' (Blackwood 1970, p9). This notion of the present and past of a subject is not the same as Pitt Rivers' claim that non-industrial societies were an opportunity to see living examples of prehistoric humans.

An emphasis on variation has taken precedence over evolutionary sequences throughout the museum. Sub-groups tend not to be overtly displayed in a particular order that could suggest a directional movement. Yet the quantity of material leads to variety in the ways it is organized. The numerous drawers are fascinating to browse through for this variety. A particular set of drawers contains a seemingly endless array of spoons and spoon-like forms, most of which are arranged in a manner that prioritizes their storage over their display. In one of these are a couple of sets of wooden spoons arranged in order to demonstrate very particular sequences of variation in design. One set comprises of a series of buildings, that gradually became more abstract. The other is made up of spoons with a decorative leaf painted upon the bowl. The anachronistic looking caption to the second series reads as follows:

Russian Peasant's spoons from Moscow shewing (sic) variation in decorative effect, due to careless painting. The outline of the central leaf design in the original becomes obscured and the red background, or interspace, loses its relationship to the leaf and becomes a dominant decorative feature. (Museum Label)

The final spoon is identified with a label that read: 'Stage shewing comlete degradation of the pattern. The lines indicating the leaf-pattern have completely disappeared, the red patch, formerly the mere interspace of the design, alone surviving'(Museum Label). This is not evolution as enforced by Pitt Rivers but rather an attempt to trace the movement of an idea, in this case a decorative pattern. The language suggests value judgement with words such as 'careless' and 'degradation' – which could easily imply Pitt Rivers' own belief in the evolutionary decline and degradation of certain cultures, but the arrangement itself is not inherently imbued with such ideology. Rather, it pieces together a process of transformation that might otherwise be invisible. The focus here is on precisely the subtle, gradual variations that Pitt Rivers aimed to highlight, but without the imposition of social evolution and the nineteenth-century ideological prejudices towards non-western cultures.

In general, the displays show some resistance to editing. As a teaching resource, the museum claims that it is attempting to provide as many examples as possible for study rather than isolating a very limited number. While the museum may have on occasion admitted to a lack of space this is not exactly a chaotic mess (Blackwood 1970, p.8). Rather it presents a mode of classificatory display that differs from familiar expectations. This is accompanied by a tone which is overtly anachronistic, giving the impression that this is a preserved specimen in suspended in formaldehyde. The artist Mark Dion, whose practice focuses on museological forms of collection and display, has made such an observation:

To me the museum embodies the 'official story' of a particular way of thinking at a particular time for a particular group of people. It is a time capsule. So I think once a museum is opened, it should remain unchanged as a window into the obsessions and prejudices of a period, like the Pitt Rivers in Oxford, the Museum of Comparative Anatomy in

Paris and the Teyler Museum in Haarlem. If someone wants to update the museum, they should build a new one. An entire city of museums would be nice, each stuck in its own time. (Kwon 1997, p.17)

Dion's perception of the Pitt Rivers Museum as a window onto another period, a structure that has remained unchanged, is romantically optimistic and clouds the view of the museum. Such places would be extraordinary, and I share his desire for keeping such preserved examples, but this museum is not one of them. While it is part of a much larger history that has shaped our own contemporary world, this is not some frozen moment of the past that holds up the thinking and preoccupations of some other historical period and of one individual. Rather it is a living, changing, growing collection. Whereas it is clear that Pitt Rivers' views are clearly racist by contemporary standards, the museum is highly sensitive towards its depiction of other cultures and subsequently the depiction of the museum itself – this includes the choice of what is sold in the souvenir shop:

> Kate White, the marketing and visitor services officer at the museum, says that they could increase profits by selling shrunken head keyrings, duvet covers and any number of other customised products, all playing on the 'exotic', 'tribal' and 'gruesome' – words used often in press coverage of the museum. But going gruesome would misrepresent the character of the collections (of which shrunken heads are only a fraction) and would present a distorted view of the cultural values of the communities from which they originate. (Vaswani, 2001, p.49)

The museum is an active site of representation that sees itself in a position of ethical responsibility. It is not a time capsule from the distant past, but very much part of the contemporary world, a highly complex, systematically arranged institution that can offer valuable insight into the understanding of our relationships with objects. This is a legacy of the Great Exhibition that is distinct from the ruins of Sydenham. The museum here was generated by the momentum of the 1851 explosion, forced backwards as it looked upon the catastrophe, the piling wreckage. Rather, the Pitt Rivers Museum offers a strand of modernity that is able to encompass and take control of what Ernst Bloch calls three dimensional temporality (1995). The museum is a site that has managed to steer, to navigate, and to control the shockwaves of modernity. This is not a fossil, or a ruin. It is a living, ethically committed form of a contemporary space of modernity and enlightenment.

Chapter 4

A Palace of Green Porcelain

Imagine yourself looking out onto a silent landscape of verdant hills and lush vegetation, punctuated by magnificent yet seemingly derelict palaces. After having embarked on a perilous journey and travelling far, perhaps further than anyone before, you have found yourself, as much by accident than design, alone in this uncharted place. This land is disturbingly strange, its alterity emphasised by the great distance traversed. Yet although different, it still has some kind of vital connection to your point of origin, and forces you to think as much of home as of the scene before you. There is an inconsistent split between familiar and strange, as if the two are overlaid, and the relative opacity and translucency of these layers reveals things known to us from our own world and remind us of other places, other stories. There are moments of recognition and legibility, despite the overwhelming mysterious peculiarity of it all. This sketch relates to a particular form of narrative contrivance. It fits into the specific tradition of utopian fiction; not so much a loosely defined genre as it is an uncanny and recurring spectre. Alternatively it could be seen as a kind of chronic hunger that nags away from within the history of social reflection. Or maybe this type of persistent fantasy could be seen as a form of that universal peculiarity of human experience and desire - the overstepping of boundaries. All of these possibilities evoke Ernst Bolch's resolute commitment to an understanding of utopia, or more specifically a utopian impulse, as a mode of observation and interpretation (Bolch, 1995).

This landscape belongs to a specific narrative of future-orientated utopian speculation. At the same time, it is also another layer of the landscape of modernity as shaped by the Great Exhibition. It is drawn from *The Time Machine*, written by H.G. Wells in 1895. (The story ran as a monthly serial in *New Review* from January to May 1895. The singular book version was also published in May 1895 by William Heinemann, publisher of *New Review*). This short novel can be defined by the ways in which not just objects, but rather a more encompassing sense of materiality has been meticulously arranged to convey a detailed, familiar environment in which a fantasy narrative can play out. This sense of a graspable everyday setting is dependent on a solidity of detailed materiality, as are the fantastic elements. This suggested quality of materiality and material culture relates not only to artefacts but also to notions of selfhood. Material culture and materiality are asserted in the text, and are manifested as a concrete presence. Addressing a novel as a space of material culture might be seen as a desire to test what might be understood by the term, a looking inwards from a vantage point located outside of its more generally-accepted dominant disciplinary forms within anthropology, archaeology and museum studies. Whereas the dominant uses and descriptive accounts of material culture as a form of knowledge and set of disciplinary concerns relate to the idea of the solid artefact I'd like to question the privileging of physical objects as the focus of material culture. This speculative notion of material culture is then, I would suggest, made available as a context with which to think about realms of material practice, objecthood, text, environment and constitutions of subjectivity.

Consistently engaged in shaping ideas relating to modes of social reform Wells's career was animated by the appearance of utopias. These both mirrored his idiosyncratic brand of socialism and stepped beyond it as his futuristic visions took their re-arrangement of society to severe extremes. Patrick Parrinder provides a more generous account of Wells's sense of social responsibility and political engagement than I have so far suggested here:

By the 1920s, Wells was not only a famous author but a public figure whose name was rarely out of the newspapers. He briefly worked for the Ministry of Propaganda in 1918, producing a memorandum on war aims which anticipated the setting-up of the League of Nations. In 1922 and 1923 he stood for Parliament as a Labour candidate. He sought to influence world leaders, including two US Presidents, Theodore Roosevelt and Franklin D. Roosevelt. His meeting with Lenin in the Kremlin in 1920 and his interview in 1934 with Lenin's successor Josef Stalin were publicized all over the world. His high-pitched piping voice was often heard on

BBC radio. In 1933 he was elected president of International PEN, the writers' organization campaigning for intellectual freedom. In the same year his books were publicly burnt by the Nazis in Berlin, and he was banned from visiting Fascist Italy. His ideas strongly influenced the Pan-European Union, the pressure group advocating European unity between the wars. (2005, p.xii)

Parrinder's emphasis on this period of Wells's life makes clear that his fantasy writing must always be read in relation to his engagement with social reality, and in particular, as engaged in a lifelong exploration of utopian impulses.

In *The Time Machine*, his first novel, he sets out to consider the worst that can happen, rather than offering an image of an ideal future. This short book was the first of a sequence - *The War of the Worlds, The Invisible Man, The Island of Dr Moreau* and *The First Men in the Moon* - written between 1895 and 1901, that he described as 'Scientific Romances'. As a formative work of modern science fiction it has an originary resonance. In particular, Wells's novel exploits that essential element that Darko Suvin argues make possible the 'basis for a coherent poetics' of science fiction: the aspect of strange newness, or novum (1979, p.4). Suvin distinguishes science fiction from other forms of fiction 'by the narrative dominance or hegemony of a fictional 'novum' (novelty, innovation) validated by cognitive logic' (1979, p.63). Wells configured his fantasies according to a very particular arrangement of cognitive logic and fictional novum, and *The Time Machine* serves as a generative model for Suvin's influential work on science fiction.

As a set of textual practices, science fiction did not appear from thin air. Sir Thomas More's *Utopia* of 1516 must share, according to Suvin, with *The Time Machine* its status as principle point of departure for modern science fiction (1979, p.222). The term 'science fiction' itself can be traced back to 1851. The

English writer William Willson, taken with the potential for modernity and technological change being brought into focus at the time, used the phrase to describe the revealing of scientific truths interwoven with narrative truths. This was a poetry of science and a poetry of life where the literary should mirror the marvel of creation. For Wilson, The Great Exhibition was a violent and spectacular revelation of radical newness that threw 'deeply into shade the old romances and fanciful legends of our boyhood' (James, 1995, p.28).

Tom Moylan employs an account of world-building as a formal and logical characteristic of the mechanics of science fiction, an 'ability to generate cognitively substantial yet estranged alternative worlds'. (2000, p.5) For Moylan, this is the greatest pleasure to be found in science fiction. However, he also argues that it is the source of its subversive potential:

(...)for if a reader can manage to see the world differently (in that Brechtian sense of overcoming alienation by becoming critically estranged and engaged), she or he might just, especially in concert with friends or comrades and allies, do something to alter it. (Moylan 2000, p.5)

Moylan's sense of world-building could be read as mutually constituted by author and reader. This mechanism of imagining an elsewhere at the same time as providing a cognitive map of contemporary actuality goes some way towards envisioning the sense of materiality that is detectable in The Time Machine.

However, to better understand the quality I wish to evoke, it is necessary to trace Wells's attempts to differentiate the Scientific Romances from the work of Jules Verne. Wells objected being compared to Verne - an objection that was mutually upheld by Verne himself. The distinction Wells makes between their works is very specific. He says of his own early novels:

As a matter of fact there is no literary resemblance whatever between the anticipatory inventions of the great Frenchman and these fantasies. His work dealt almost always with actual possibilities of invention and discovery, and he made some remarkable forecasts. The interest he invoked was a practical one; he wrote and believed and told that this or that thing could be done, which was not at that time done. He helped his reader to imagine it done to realise what fun, excitement or mischief would ensue. Many of his inventions have 'come true'. (Wells 1933, p.vii)

In contrast, Wells describes the Scientific Romances as fantasies. Rather than projecting a conceivable possibility their conviction is analogous to that of a dream. After reading one of these novels one wakes up to its impossibility. However, these are dreams that may not relate to technological possibility, but certainly relate to social possibility. The dream is one that takes place within a recognised and politicised configuration of social reality, which it offers a contrast to. Like that of William Guest, the protagonist and somnambulant time traveller in William Morris's *News from Nowhere* (1890), the dream Wells describes is one of a possible future experienced from the present.

Wells describes the 'living interest' of these novels as lying in the non-fantastic elements: '(...) the fantastic element, the strange property or the strange world, is used only to throw up and intensify our natural reactions of wonder, fear or perplexity' (1933, p.viii). The invention in itself is nothing, it is only the translation of a singular fantastic element into a commonplace world that invests the narrative with the values of literary interest and engagement that Wells describes as 'human'. It is essential to isolate the fantastic, to restrict it to a singular contrivance. Wells' logic is predicated on the possibility of identification, of the sense of readers projecting themselves into the fictional circumstance and asking what might happen to them if they were in this situation:

> But no one would think twice about the answer if hedges and
> houses also began to fly, or if people changed into lions,
> tigers, cats and dogs left and right, or if everyone could
> vanish anyhow. Nothing remains interesting where anything
> may happen. (1933, p.viii)

There is a correlation with Wells' rules for what constitutes the
interest value in his scientific romances in Suvin's assertion that
science fiction can be usefully thought of as the literature of
cognitive estrangement.

This category is held up in contrast to narratives of pure
fantasy, such as the folktale:

> The stock folktale accessory, such as the flying carpet, evades
> the empirical law of physical gravity – as the hero evades
> social gravity – by imagining its opposite. This wish-fulfilling
> element is its strength and its weakness, for it never pretends
> that a carpet could be expected to fly – that a humble third
> son could be expected to become king – while there is a
> gravity. (Suvin 1979, p.8)

In attempting a rigorous understanding of science fiction as a
category of literature Suvin's example binds a specificity of
literary form to a particular relationship with materiality. I would
like to read Suvin's emphasis on the conditions in which
cognitive estrangement can usefully take place within literatures
of the fantastic as a means of interpreting a connection between a
crude sense of material possibility and social possibility, which
seems latent in Wells's early utopia - a more believable constitution of materiality and its inherent potential for transformation
in text suggests a more profound impulse for change in the mind
of the reader.

In his own account of the scientific romances Wells' own trick was to domesticate the impossible. A plausible illusion allows the story to play out, and science becomes a modern substitute for magic, which Wells thought had lost its narrative currency by the late nineteenth century: 'I simply brought the fetish stuff up to date, and made it as near actual theory as possible' (1933, p.viii). This desire to renew the conventions of fantasy was itself, nothing new, as the same desire prompted Shelley to make Victor Frankenstein a scientist, purely as a means of differentiating her story from the tired conventions of Gothic Romance (Stableford 1995, p.54). But aside from the presence of trickery, Wells sees the business of the fantasy writer as maintaining a sense of reality: 'Touches of prosaic detail are imperative and a rigorous adherence to the hypothesis. Any extra fantasy outside the cardinal assumption immediately gives a touch of irresponsible silliness to the invention' (1933, p.ix). Used in this precise way, fantasy holds the potential, in Wells' argument, to provide a new and novel angle on telling stories which themselves might be discursively revealing. Wells admits the presence of his admiration for Swift's *Gulliver's Travels* throughout the Scientific Romances as a profound influence, 'and it is particularly evident in a predisposition to make the stories reflect upon contemporary political and social discussions' (1933, p.ix).

Writing soon after Wells' death, Jorge Luis Borges writes that Wells 'bestowed sociological parables with a lavish hand' (Parrinder 1972, p.332). Yet it is Borges' own poem *Things* that might be equally appropriate in characterising the Scientific Romances:

My cane, my pocket change, this ring of keys,
The obedient lock, the belated notes,
The few days left to me will not find time
To read, the deck of cards, the table-top,

A book encrushed in its pages the withered
Violet, monument to an afternoon
Undoubtedly unforgettable, now forgotten,
the mirror in the west where a red sunrise
blazes its illusion. How many things,
files, doorsills, atlases, nails,
serve us like slaves who never say a word,
blind and so mysteriously reserved.
They will endure beyond our vanishing;
And they will never know that we have gone.
(Hawkins and Olsen 2003, p.xvii)

Borges thematizes a range and scope of material culture beyond any simplistic notions that artefacts carry semiotic meanings. Rather the poem suggests that notions of self are bound up with seemingly trivial, but invasively intimate, things. Similarly, I would like to suggest that while *The Time Machine* is a utopian discourse of social conflict and possibility, it also constitutes a sense of materiality. It needs to be stressed that this quality is not limited to definitions of relationships with things but, as in Borges' poem, materiality concerns the nature of subjects, rather than merely a static notion of objects.

As a story *The Time Machine* is elegant, precise and efficient: Hillyer, the narrator, or more appropriately, the 'outer narrator', is a friend and regular guest of the central protagonist. Referred to only as 'the Time Traveller', he could be described as the 'inner narrator', whose account is contained within the outer narration. Hillyer's narration begins with a scene in the Time Traveller's home, where in front of an audience of guests, the Time Traveller attempts to describe a speculative theory of time as the fourth dimension. He then reveals a miniature but fully operational time machine. Before the assembled guests, the machine vanishes, to a suspicious and incredulous response. After stating his intention of travelling in time, he shows to his guests the actual machine housed in his workshop, not yet complete. The following week, another group of guests, which includes Hillyer, have assembled at the Time Traveller's house. They wait impatiently as their host has not yet arrived, and sit down to dinner without him. Suddenly, the Time Traveller makes a dramatic entrance, demanding food and drink, disturbingly haggard in appearance. He explains that he has been to the future and from this point; the 'inner narrator' takes over as he relates the events of his journey. That morning, he had tried out his machine in a reckless and unprepared leap into the future, arriving in the year 802,701.

The future world that he encounters is a landscape punctuated by ruined, palatial structures and populated by the descendants of late nineteenth-century humans. After this huge period of time, humanity has evolved into two distinguishable species: The Eloi and the Morlocks. The Eloi are regarded by the Time Traveller as beautiful, androgynous, physically frail, and as intellectually regressive. All their material needs are catered for by the subterranean, ape-like Morlocks. As the Time Traveller eventually deduces the Eloi are cattle reared by the Morlocks as food. The Time Traveller also discovers that his machine has vanished, dragged inside the base of a statue by Morlocks, and its recovery becomes the focus of the Time Traveller's activities in the future. During his stay, he befriends an Eloi named Weena. Assuming she is female, their relationship verges on romance. However, despite his best efforts to protect her, she is lost during a confrontation with the Morlocks, and is presumed dead. He eventually succeeds in finding the machine and makes a frantic escape, accidentally hurtling even further into the future. He finds himself on the shore of a sea in a world that continually faces a static and bloated red sun, watching the final generations of the last forms of life on earth. This scene of a grotesque sunset populated by bizarre creatures is literally the twilight of the earth and its life.

The Time Traveller then begins his return journey.

Upon his return, the voice of the novel then switches back to the 'outer narrator' Hillyer. After the Time Traveller tells his story to an entertained but unconvinced audience, Hillyer returns the following day, unable to reconcile himself to the story as a mere invention or delusion. He meets the Time Traveller, with a camera and knapsack, apparently preparing for another journey. Hillyer is asked to wait for him, but manages by chance to see the faint image of the time machine disappearing, the Time Traveller an indistinct figure in a whirling mass as he disappears. Hillyer explains in his account that he waited at the Time Traveller's house for his return but then feared that he would have to wait a lifetime, and that three years had now passed. As an epilogue, Hillyer imagines what could have become of his friend, comforted by two shrivelled white flowers of an unknown order, material evidence brought back from the future.

The population encountered in the year 802,701 are described according to grotesquely exaggerated physiognomic principles. Their bodies are codified to suggest their species characteristics, the historical struggle which has been the cause of their evolution and that has led to this cannibalistic resolution, is firmly rooted in Wells's present. The differentiation of their physiology is unambiguously rendered: the Morlocks as ape-like beasts in contrast to the fragility of the Eloi, their features described as a 'Dresden china type of prettiness', beautiful but infantile (Wells 1895, p.33). This quality of the Eloi, which is more than sexual and actually accounts for a whole form of society, is contrasted with The Time Traveller's impressions of the Morlocks:

> I felt a peculiar shrinking from those pallid bodies. They were just the half-bleached colour of the worms and things one see preserved in spirit in a zoological museum. And they were

filthily cold to the touch. Probably my shrinking was largely due to the sympathetic influence of the Eloi, whose disgust of the Morlocks I now began to appreciate. (Wells 1895, p.86)

These radical differences between the two species, one inducing 'peculiar shinking', the other 'sympathetic influence', are both physiological and indications of character, and the distinct responses described by the Time Traveller seem to be generated and sustained as a mutual effect. The split that constitutes these radically contrasting species has been brought about by some form of evolutionary principle but this is not something that can be accounted for as strictly the result of a purely Darwinian process of selection and adaptation, but rather, as the Time Traveller eventually hypothesises, has been brought about by perpetuation of social conditions that exist within his own epoch. This transformation of bodies is purely physiognomic. These descriptions seem to mark a distinct sense of contrast between rational, classificatory discourses associated with specimens from a zoological museum, and both the Eloi and Morlocks: as races whose cultures are embodied in their physical forms, and whose cultures are incapable of supporting something as complex as museological activity. They are therefore clearly both differentiated from the form of humanity represented by the Time Traveller. This cultural alterity, embodied in difference of species, is reinforced subsequently by the discovery of the Palace of Green Porcelain, an abandoned ruin of a vast museum, that retains none of its original significance to either Eloi or Morlock. Yet this museum also introduces a pseudo-scientific perspective on these bodies, through a suggestion of scientific objectivity, and an associative connection between physiognomy and rational classificatory discourses. While from a rational, late nineteenth-century perspective, such an emphasis on physiognomy appears irrational and in opposition to any scientific, classificatory discourse, assumptions based on appearance are deeply rooted and persistent long beyond the point of Wells's writing of *The Time Machine*.

Physiognomy in its loosest sense has been a historically enduring set of ideas, and appears to be as old as recorded culture. It is arguably described as a fundamental and a universally cross-cultural issue, in the sense that it is concerned with relationships between the outward appearances of an embodied subject, and some culturally assigned values located within. Its perceptual assumptions find voice in Socrates and Plato, in the certainty of an un-coincidental propinquity of vice and ugliness, and physical beauty reflecting inner beauty respectively: '(Socrates) would advise youths to look in their mirrors every morning to note what progress they were making along the path of virtue' (Tytler 1982, p.36). Aristotle's *Physiognomonica*, which until the eighteenth century was generally regarded as the standard work on physiognomy, relied upon symmetry and proportion as a register of moral disposition. While its systematic tabulation gives the appearance of believable solidity there are more incredulous parallels drawn between human and animal naturei.e. the qualities of a lion depict properties of masculinity, and a panther femininity. Yet despite the persistence of a connection between outward appearance and inner self, the idea of physiognomy was most clearly articulated and popularised as a rational and scientific form in the late eighteenth century by the Swiss theologian, philosopher and physiologist Johann Caspar Lavater. His work, with its reliance on painfully detailed rules concerning the smallest details of physical appearance, was often confused with phrenology, and the two fields were viewed as extremely close, often indistinguishably so, in the nineteenth century.

The nineteenth century novel as a general form shares an unshakeable link to Lavater's physiognomic writings, in particular, his *Physiognomische Fragmente* (1775-8). This is revealed by the popularity of physiognomy as a credible discourse between the 1770s and 1880s. However, by the end of the nineteenth century, modes of rationalist and empiricist thought had largely dispelled the scientific appearance of physiological disciplines, in part, due to the discrediting of phrenology, which although distinct, appeared as a specific science of a general principle. Wells, as a former student of science, had no actual commitment to physiognomy as a reliable principle, but rather *The Time Machine*, like the other Scientific Romances, is a self-conscious and deliberate engagement with physiognomy at an allegorical level, rather than an attempt to perpetuate a literal concurrence with the correlation of appearance and character. This Lavater-influenced approach should be read as a device; a literary conceit rather than a literal reflection and reproduction of ideology.

The bodies of humanity's future, the distinct species of Eloi and Morlock can be characterised in terms of degeneration. The idea of the embodied ruination of the human subject is prevalent in British fiction at the turn of the century, and is particularly evident in the gothic and fantastic. The bodies in *The Time Machine* are consistent with this notion of a loose set of genre concerns and strategies, in which human subjects are defamiliarised and violently reconstituted within the text. Such fictional and alarmist re-articulations of embodied subjectivity can be placed within a general set of anxieties around notions of degeneration, which by the end of the nineteenth century were prevalent and concrete in their manifestations. Such anxieties are well described by Max Nordau's *Degeneration* (1893; English trans. 1895). Nordau's ideas are descended from those of Cesare Lombroso, whose fame comes from his investigations of criminal anthropology and in particular his theory of the 'born criminal'. For Lombroso, criminal behaviour was understandable in terms of atavism, or rather how latent characteristics from earlier points of species history might reappear. The form of the physical body revealed with readable precision the intellectual, moral and emotional nature of the subject. Criminality was therefore innate and recognisable as a set of varied physical characteristics. These were absent from a normative model of the Caucasian western subject, but present in the form of features such as an irregular cranium, an asymmetrical face, large ears or disproportionate limbs.

These anomalies to the normative body were signs of reversion to earlier stages in humanity's evolutionary development as a species as well as finding analogous comparisons with other species. While an obvious comparison might be thought to have been drawn up with apes, Lombroso's list of physical correspondences is drawn from an extensive and absurdly inconsistent selection of possible ancestral forms, including: 'dogs, rodents, lemurs, reptiles, oxen, birds of prey, and domestic fowl, to name a few' (Hurley 1996, p.93). These traces could be found across the whole exterior of a body, as well as inside e.g. in abnormalities of brain structure. Their presence in humans did not itself cause criminal behaviour, but did reveal a savage or animal-like set of characteristics within a subject that were likely to prompt acts of criminal behaviour, which might generally be thought of as a beast-like transgression of civilized restraint and morality. Kelly Hurley's reading of Lombroso's atavism is a description of a type of embodied subjectivity which is too full of varied and incompatible histories. This is a reading of human bodies that is potentially 'utterly chaotic, unable to maintain its distinctions from a whole world of animal possibilities' (Hurley 1996, p.94). As a student and zealous advocate of Lombroso, Nordau sought to convey, through a specificity of investigated form, a sense of urgency in his argument concerning the snowballing perpetuation of decadence as a genuine threat to civilization. Tendencies in art and literature offered proof of the degeneracy of their authors, and the enthusiasm of their admirers was proof of insanity and imbecility

(Nordau 1995, p.vii). Nordau's views on progress were built upon the redemptive potential of the natural sciences. Humanity's future can only lie in its elevation and development, based upon a form of progress which is inseparable from rational scientific thought.

If the differences between the two future sub-species have been brought about by some form of evolutionary principle, the nature of this principle is indicated by the image of the Sphinx that dominates the immediate landscape around the Time Traveller's point of arrival, and inside which his machine is later hidden by Morlocks (Stover 1996). The statue alludes to an essay by Thomas Carlyle from his collection *Past and Present* (1843), which together with his *Sartor Resartus* (1838) – referred to by the Time Traveller - was ubiquitously familiar to Wells's late nineteenth-century audience. The degree of Carlyle's fame is demonstrated in Conan Doyle's *A Study in Scarlet* (1887) as Watson, the narrator, describes his bewilderment at his new acquaintance, Sherlock Holmes. While his knowledge of some fields was astoundingly extensive, there seemed to be some radical gaps in Holmes's field of learning:

> His ignorance was as remarkable as his knowledge. Of contemporary literature, philosophy and politics he appeared to know next to nothing. Upon my quoting Thomas Carlyle, he inquired in the naïvest way who he might be and what he had done. (Conan Doyle 2003, p13)

The radical inconsistencies in Holmes's knowledge mean that he also has no knowledge of the structure or planets of the Solar System which is also described as a comparison to put the strangeness of his ignorance of Carlyle into perspective.

Carlyle's essay draws upon the allegory of the Sphinx. This concerns the myth that certain death was promised to anyone that could not answer her riddle. The essay prophesied a similar fate if his question relating to the organisation of labour and management of the working classes were to remain unanswered. For Carlyle, decadent generations of factory owners had allowed labour to organize itself with ''ape's freedom' in pursuit of sectarian class interests at the expense of social duty; with the 'liberty of apes', Labour seeks its own greed no less than its nominal masters given only to profiteering' (Stover 1996, p.3). Carlyle's solution to this unsustainable system was the militarising of Labour. In Wells's future, this problem has been allowed to escalate, giving his fear of an organised working class bestial and predatory materiality. Stover makes the point that in recognising his own social context, 'the Time Traveller realizes that he has never left home; that the future is but a mockery of his own time' (1996, p.2).

If the Morlocks are apes, an inverted physiognomy applies to the Eloi. Their name is the plural version of Elohim, who in the Olds Testament are lesser Canaanite gods, self appointed, doomed to failure. Wells's Eloi are heirs to generations of ruling classes whose actions have led to degeneration and destructive failure. They are the ruling class subjects at which Carlyle aims his discourse. More specifically, they are the leisure class, Dandies living for show on the surface of life, while Drudges dig and labour in the earth, denied glimpses of the sky. It is this social discourse, transformed into an embodied habitus, that determines the evolutionary development of the future, rather than Darwinian adaptation.

Yet the status of these bodies, as human or not, is consistently unresolved and ambiguous. This indeterminacy, in part, seems to be articulated by Judith Butler's sense of bodies as being subject to materialization through discursive performativity (1993). The future world is one that disrupts the Foucaultian regulatory ideals that Butler argues constitute sexual difference and the stability of an embodied subject. Within such regulatory practices is, according to Butler, a kind of productive form of power that is able to produce the bodies it controls. In a sense, the perspective of the Time Traveller might also constitute such a power, one that is attempting to both make sense of, and simultaneously constitute, the bodies he encounters. This process of constitution is not physical, but involves the interpretation of their corporeality within a system of moral and socially explicable matrices. This correlates initially to appearance, but also to behaviour, and perhaps ultimately, when coming to the conclusion of murderous desire and the right to life, seems determined by propinquity or distance to his notion of humanness.

Uncertainty characterises the body of the narrative itself, in a form that is more fundamental than a mere thematic tendency within the descriptions of the embodied subjects themselves. As a social medium in which the construction of bodies may occur, it is full of the qualities set out by Hurley as forms of abhuman physicality, a spectacle of undifferentiated forms metamorphic states of existence. Hurley describes fin-de-siècle Gothic as a set of accounts of interstitial becomings, of metamorphoses and indifferentiation, as human bodies between species. As a fin-de-siècle Gothic narrative that is simultaneously a on degeneration, the 'gothicity' of *The Time Machine* is one that is rendered, I would suggest, as a doubled image. Hurley suggests that degeneration itself is not so much a stable, objective and scientific form, but is one that is already gothic in character. By elevating this characteristic narrative element of fin-de-siècle Gothic to the status of the novel's most overt thematic concern Wells presents us with a text that is uniquely reflexive as a form of gothic discourse. Not only is its character one that is rendered by the qualities of the abhuman that the fin-de-siècle Gothic is most exemplified by, but is itself an openly critical form of discourse on those very qualities as articulated by broader discussions of degeneration.

The forms of time and temporality in *The Time Machine* are

identifiable as manifestations of materiality and material culture. One such convergence is in the discourse of evolution, and the museological discourse identified in the novel, which exemplify the organisation of temporal representations through architecture and display. As perhaps a material form in itself, and certainly an element of the material world that the novel constitutes, time might be seen here as definable by its susceptibility to analysis and ultimately through its apprehension and realisation as a navigable substance. Likewise, the invention of the time machine itself serves to transform pre-Einsteinian time, into something that has both spatial substance and historical resonance. The most certain, yet utterly ambiguous, point on which the novel rests is the eponymous machine itself, a dramatic contrivance that Wells has introduced into his mimetic and concrete reality.

In *The Time Machine*, there is no attempt to explain how such a device might work, nor is there a detailed account of the appearance of the machine. Instead, this central object is described in terms of a few loose details. This does not seem accidental, as the attendance to one would necessitate the elaboration of the other. Specifying particular components would indicate operational instrumentality of some kind. It is impossible to discern whether the machine is constructed from a novel configuration of existing technologies, or if it relies on as yet unimagined agency. Its appearance is unfamiliar to the narrator, borne out by his inability to provide an adequate account or a suitable comparative image. Its form is also of sufficient complexity to defy a straightforward description. A relatively comprehensive account of the machine actually refers to the working scale model used in a demonstration to an audience of assembled guests who meet at the Time Traveller's home:

The thing the Time Traveller held in his hand was a glittering metallic framework, scarcely larger that a small clock, and very delicately made. There was ivory in it, and some transparent crystalline substance. (Wells 1895, p.10)

The sense of what this object is comes across as vague and its purpose utterly obscure. It is described only indirectly, in terms of its scale and the quality of its construction. There is a hint of some mysterious technology at work but this is not developed. Rather, the workmanship of the model is emphasised. The model is imbued with a sense of its value due to the recognition of the labour and temporal investment required to make the piece, together with the skilled use of seductive materials. This value is illuminated and accentuated by the sacrifice that is required by the act of demonstrating its operational function. The sacrificial aspect of the demonstration, involving the irretrievable loss of the model time machine, is made more poignant in the narrative by the incredulous reactions of the witnesses, which ultimately renders the performance as a display of irrational expenditure.

After the demonstration with the model, the actual machine is revealed, but little more is given away relating to how it functions or its appearance. The parts are suggestive of a machine with complex and finely crafted components and, as materials, have an odd, domestic familiarity. The Time Traveller's guests are also taken to see the machine after his return, although this time it is more to reassure himself than his audience of the veracity of his story. It bears damage and evidential traces that appear to corroborate his tale:

There in the flickering light of the lamp was the machine sure enough, squat, ugly, and askew; a thing of brass, ebony, ivory, and translucent glimmering quartz. Solid to the touch – for I put out my hand and felt the rail of it – and with brown spots and smears upon the ivory, and bits if grass and moss upon the lower parts, and one rail bent awry.

The Time Traveller put the lamp down on the bench, and
ran his hand along the damaged rail. (Wells 1895, pp.147-148)

Little more is revealed of it, except through fragments that build,
incrementally constituting the qualitative presence of this
machine. The vagueness of the form of the machine itself is a
necessity, facilitating the introduction of an unknown
technology as a narrative device. *The Time Machine* can be seen as
a formative point in the process of imagining technologies which
remain ambiguous yet are compiled out of a constructed set of
generalities and specificities. How else could this form of
technology be conceptualised except through such a balance of
vagueness and recognition? The play within this chain of
signification relies upon a general familiarity with the specific
differences between each signifying mark.

The machine generates associations with clocks, with
bicycles, something of a middle-class craze in the 1890s and one
that was in Wells' view utopian in its technological promise, and
proto-cinematic apparatuses. All of these are modern formswith
an edge of radical novelty in the 1890s. However, from a
contemporary perspective the machine enters into the field of
influence of antique objects. Not only does it do so on account of
its age, but also due to the material elements described. Brass,
ebony and ivory assume a quality of temporal otherness to a
contemporary perspective that is evocative of historical
furniture and interiors. This is an ambivalent status. Regardless
of the technological arrangements of substances into machine
forms, the presence of these materials alone within the text
suggests an advanced moment of modernity, dependent on the
technological processes of their production or refinement, and
on structures of colonialism and international commerce that
would ensure their availability. These materials fluctuate
between their status as contemporary, nineteenth-century
technology, and their evoking of antique objects. But ultimately

they gravitate towards modernity, as a complex of technological sophistication and a process of movement encompassed by the overarching structure of Empire, a spectre that haunts the novel as a material world.

There is a particular discovery made by the Time Traveller that relates specifically to ideas of materiality and material culture. This is the so-called Palace of Green Porcelain. Shortly after entering the vast building, The Time Traveller declares the Palace to be in fact a museum: 'Clearly (says the time traveller) we stood among the ruins of some latter-day South Kensington!' (Wells 1895, p.108). This is a monument to the nineteenth century, carried out in some far-distant era that still precedes the age of Eloi. As a super-museum, it represents a culmination of civilization on a temporal scale, as well as the site for its organization and interpretation. More than this it signifies without ambiguity the distant moment of such an apex. These remains suggest that the age of progress is long over. All that remains are decaying ruins. The image is one not of the height of Empire and Victorian culture, but its distant and fantastical futurity as a failed civilisation, long since vanished. There remain material traces upon which to gaze and reflect.

The Time Traveller's citing of South Kensington is an unambiguous reference to what is now known as the Victoria and Albert Museum in London. The South Kensington Museum opened in 1881, just two years before Wells started at the Normal School of Science, which was just across the road from where Imperial College is today, and which was to become a constituent part of Imperial. It was here that Wells studied under Thomas Huxley, and it was the evolutionist Huxley who finally discredited Richard Owen, through publicly debating Darwin's work and ridiculing Owen's Creationist tendencies. The museum itself grew, of course, out of the aftermath of the Great Exhibition, held in nearby Hyde Park, while the entire topography of South Kensington was transformed as

Albertopolis, looked upon by the giant golden statue on his memorial throne. However, the growth of institutions in this area was as much to do with the anxiety brought about by a lack of favourable comparison in the international arena, as it was by any notions of progressive optimism. A general but dire shortcoming was identified by holding Britain's material culture up to that of the rest of the world as it was represented. The South Kensington Museum was a concrete manifestation of the need to respond to this anxiety.

The Palace of Green Porcelain is one of several buildings explored by the Time Traveller and described as 'palaces', due to their overblown scale. As all of these buildings are described as 'living palaces', and seem to be filled only with dining halls and sleeping chambers, the museological status of the Palace of Green Porcelain comes as a great surprise to the Time Traveller, but is actually signposted from the outset of its appearance. Like the Palace of Green Porcelain, the Crystal Palace was also a form of super-museum that played out history as a vast but mappable evolutionary structure. Upon first seeing the Palace of Green Porcelain, it is made clear that this is unlike any other structure that the Time Traveller has encountered in the future:

> It was larger than the largest of the palaces or ruins I knew, and the façade had an Oriental look: the face of it having the lustre, as well as the pale-green tint, a kind of bluish green, of a certain type of Chinese porcelain. This difference in aspect suggested a difference in use(...) (Wells 1895, p.88)

The image is one that fits well with what the view would have been like of the Crystal Palace as it stood on Sydenham Hill.

The temporality suggested by the presence of the Palace of Green Porcelain, and its status as a fantasised version of the Crystal Palace, is not straightforward. Perhaps the most vocal, and sustained, critic of the Crystal Palace's life span from its initial construction, to its permanent relocation, was John Ruskin. If Carlyle's arguments as they are unambiguously presented within The Time Machine can be summarised as the 'Riddle of the Sphinx', then I would like to suggest that Ruskin may also be introduced, albeit more speculatively, under the general banner of *The Seven Lamps of Architecture* (1849). The disdain Ruskin demonstrated for the Crystal Palace, which he dismissed as neither made from crystal, nor a palace, might also offer some reflections on the Palace of Green Porcelain. Architecture, for Ruskin, was not merely a formal practice, but an issue of constructing stability in the face of rapid change, of moral continuity, or social reform. Buildings had to be addressed in terms of responsibility to aesthetics, a realm that encompassed the political and social, meaning and morality. His work owed much to that of Carlyle, whose writings he reread and assimilated into his mode of thought. Drawing on a comparative approach between modernity and a fantasised medieval past, Ruskin, through the lens of Carlyle, sought to draw distinct combinations of past and present to highlight an urgent need of reform in the face of fragmentation and a dangerous lack of social cohesion. This perspective is reflected and inverted in the discourse of *The Time Machine*, looking to the future to articulate the apparent dangers and anxieties of the present.

The Crystal Palace became a central motif in Ruskin's comparative method standing in for all the distorted thinking of his own era. It was an alienated form, and one cut off from his idealised synthesis of categories that would bring together art and nature, labour and design, as well as function and beauty. Perhaps more significant is what Ruskin saw as the blankness of the Crystal Palace. This blankness was due partially to Ruskin's idea that it was impossible to determine any sense of natural beauty or ornamentation in the repetitive iron and glass elements that through sheer seriality made up the vast building.

But the blankness was also a historical one, detached from time, history and memory. The muteness of the Crystal Palace therefore was a temporal silence as well, and one that failed to announce its connection to history. The Palace of Green Porcelain is similarly mute, revealing little of historical value as an enormous and silent ruin. It represents a complete detachment from history and memory, in a manner analogous to Ruskin's disdain for the Crystal Palace, an erasing of the past by the sheen of novelty. The Eloi are a people without history, their ruins being the ruins of a modernity that refused to relate history. The Palace of Green Porcelain as a building negates history and memory presenting a perpetual continuity of the present in the Eloi world. The alleged transparency of crystal has been replaced by the opacity of porcelain.

Yet for Ruskin, Paxton's building was far from transparent. The distant view of the Palace of Green Porcelain, as seen by the Time Traveller, brings to mind the visual obstruction that the Crystal Palace provided for Ruskin when relocated to Sydenham, near Ruskin's home in Herne Hill, South London. While actually blocking his view, Ruskin complained that the obstruction could be sustained metaphorically so that it might be said to block his ability to think about architectural history. The Crystal Palace obstructed the very shadow of the past upon the present. In medieval architecture, Ruskin could find traces of meaning, of quality, in the stones, in textured fragments.

Ruskin's despair with the form of the Crystal Palace seems not only based upon his inability to see beyond it to the architecture of the past, but also an inability to look through its glass walls, which he saw as horrifically opaque, upon its contents. Pugin's Mediaeval Court, given top billing in the Great Exhibition and at Sydenham, was as a gothic form was no less than an articulation of that very connection with the past that Ruskin deemed necessary. In its first incarnation, the Crystal Palace was a hyper-modern structure that housed within itself a set of continuities through the presence of gothic discourses in architecture and design. Specifically, these tendencies were characterised by the term Gothic Revival, later exemplified by Scott's Albert Memorial as a Victorian fantasy of temporal continuity. Gothic Revival was a set of ideas that looked to a medieval past, but unlike the historicist reiterations of popular forms of classical and Renaissance style Gothic Revival was a tradition of modernity which constructed a past and a set of traditions for itself.

For the Crystal Palace, from the point of its inauguration, to contain within it as content much material that could be characterised as Gothic Revival, suggests a situation far more complex than Ruskin is able to read into its looming presence. Its radical newness is simultaneously a model of continuous and evolutionary history. The Palace of Green Porcelain is its unambiguously rendered successor in the distant future, now abandoned as a decaying ruin. Its green surface, described as so different from the material surfaces of every other building encountered by the Time Traveller, is suggestive of the radical alterity of the Crystal Palace in its architectural context, clearly alien to all other buildings in both scale and facture. That the Crystal Palace occupies a formative place in Wells's make up is revealed by a reference in his autobiography. It appears as a site of influence on the childish but formative dawning of his sexuality (Parinder 1995, p.85). Yet the most specific character of the Crystal Palace as a structure of temporality is to be found in its content after the Great Exhibition, as a form of originary but ecstatically distorted museum. The Crystal Palace is rendered as a material and historical form within the text of *The Time Machine*. It is present as the shadow of the Great Exhibition, as Albertopolis, and as the Palace in Sydenham. The meaning of the building, though, is contradictory. It is both Ruskin's erasure of history in the blankness of surface, yet it offers a form of translation between the novel's present, recent history and far flung future.

For Wells, the dinosaurs of the Crystal Palace were already obsolete. Their configuration having been long since modified by research since the mid 1850s, these recreations of pre-history were already fossils. One of these former star attractions even makes an appearance in the novel *Kipps* (1905), likened by the eponymous protagonist to his former boss. However, palaeontology still possessed a radical status in its depiction of deep temporality, and the fossil, perhaps, was just as radical a tool for Wells as it was for Benjamin. The Palace of Green Porcelain itself is the ultimate fossil encountered by the Time Traveller, made explicit by his initial entrance to the building and the first impressions gained of the Palace as a museum:

> Here, apparently, was the Palaeontological Section, and a very splendid array of fossils it must have been, through the inevitable process of decay that had been staved off for a time, and had, through the extinction of bacteria and fungi, lost ninety-nine hundredths of its force, was, nevertheless, with extreme sureness if with extreme slowness at work again upon all its treasures. Here and there I found traces of the little people in the shape of rare fossils broken to pieces or threaded in strings upon reeds. (Wells 1895, pp.108-109)

The fossils present extinct forms, earlier orders that have long since disappeared. This, of course, is the fate of human civilization itself in this far-off future. Yet as well as offering a dire warning, the fossil can also be read as the means of reading, with a critical impulse, the structures of history. In this case, however, it seems as if hysterical polemics have dominated the kind of rupture of myth suggested by Benjamin's reading of industrial fossils.

The relation between this museological department and the notion of the fossil is two-fold. It is comprised of the fossilised bones of long extinct animals. In addition, however, the very technologies of display that transform these indexical remains into a discursive structure of history and display have also attained the condition of fossils. The gallery and its contents have been subject to processes of decay and transformation. The Time Traveller describes, as working with extreme slowness, evidence of the natural ravages of time having destroyed most of the exhibits. Yet there has been another order of destructive intervention, detectable through inscription upon the scene, as traces upon the surface of a fossil. Both the Eloi and Morlocks receive blame for depleting the collection. It is further evidence of the decadent stupidity of one race, and the wanton barbarism of the other. The Morlocks are accused of having 'bodily removed' entire cases, for some unknown purpose. The Eloi, being beyond actual purpose, are merely charged with mindless and accidental damage making jewellery from fragments of the collection. Not only are they ignorant of the knowledge within the Palace of Green Porcelain, both races have actively contributed to the destruction of history in the future.

By the 1890s, the kinds of gallery which the Time Traveller finds as a ruin were well established sites of educative spectacle. The Palace of Green Porcelain retains this sense of pedagogical narrative through visual and spatial articulation. Wells' super-museum is the climatic pinnacle of such enterprises, as described by Patrick Parrinder, who suggests that the exotic fascination conjured by dinosaurs plays a specific role in their representation of a dethroned order. By representing dinosaurs as extinct forms, they are precursors to the empire of human mastery, embodied by the order of the museum (Parrinder 1995, p.55). Wells' Palace, however, situates such self-assured dominance within the same realm of obsolete order, of extinct and failed empire:

Wells was not the only nineteenth-century writer to respond

to the fascination of these museums. Jules Verne's Captain Nemo has his own museum aboard the submarine Nautilus, while Herman Melville's Moby Dick, with its exhaustive discussions of the whale and cetological science, itself resembles nothing so much as a vast museum. Melville's explanation that 'To produce a mighty book, you must choose a mighty theme' may also explain why the great, exotic animals such as whales and dinosaur contribute so powerfully to the appeal of natural history museums. They represent alternatives to human mastery which, however, have been dethroned. (Parrinder 1995, p.55)

While Parrinder situates natural history museums within a Wellsian context as centres of propaganda for evolutionary theory this perspective fails to take into account the role of the Crystal Palace as just such a site for the construction and dissemination of evolutionary ideology.

Perhaps this is due to the complex and contradictory forces that comprised ideas of evolution, and that as an ideological device evolution was contested and less than stable. Richard Owen's championing of the prehistoric and invention of the dinosaur, distinct from any other animal ever known, reinforced his opposition to the principle of evolution, an opposition inscribed in the decorative animals that populate the façade of the Alfred Waterhouse's building that houses the Natural History Museum. The apparently random mixture of contemporary, prehistoric and mythic creatures is a deliberately provocative attempt to disavow any notion of an evolutionary progress of animals. Architectural decoration illustrated a dead end, a static temporality. Despite the complicated variations in the evolutionary discourses which give structure to the Palace of Green Porcelain, the ambiguities rendered by Owen's resistance to Darwin's teleological threat does little to stifle the evolutionary nature of Wells's Palace in the light of that of

Sydenham.

The rebuilt Crystal Palace looked upon the visible domain as its own spectacle, and therefore as included within its own narratives. The panoramic landscape and all that it contained was held in the discourse of the display. This was unprecedented on such a scale as a public, commercial, entertainment. The sprawling, expansive and mutated nature of the new Crystal Palace was reflective of this attempt to encompass as much as possible. The technology of the panoramic display at Sydenham is that of selection, the technology of the museological. This technology, the scale and the overwhelming diversity of the Crystal Palace is mirrored in Wells' fossilised equivalent from the future. There is much more to the Palace of Green Porcelain than the paleontological displays among which the Time Traveller initially finds himself:

> To judge from the size of the place, this palace of Green Porcelain had a great deal more in it than a Gallery of Palaeontology; possibly historical galleries; it might be, even a library! To me, at least in my present circumstances, these would be vastly more interesting than this spectacle of old-time geology in decay. Exploring, I found another short gallery running transversely to the first. This appeared to be devoted to minerals(.) (Wells 1895, pp.109-110)

As his exploration continues, he passes quickly through the mineralogy displays, and enters into another hall running parallel to the first one he had entered containing the remains of prehistoric fossils. While recognising its original designation, this gallery is described as 'ruinous':

> Apparently this section had been devoted to natural history, but everything had long since passed out of recognition. A few shrivelled and blackened vestiges of what had once been

stuffed animals, desiccated mummies in jars that had once held spirit, a brown dust of departed plants: that was all! (Wells 1895, p.110)

The Time Traveller expresses regret at the condition of the remains of this collection, as he ' should have been glad to trace the patient re-adjustments by which the conquest of animated nature had been attained' (Wells 1895, p.110). He is denied the visualisation of incremental and, ultimately, progressive change by the overwhelming force of evolutionary and temporal power in the novel - degeneration.

The Palace also offers another form of remarkable conflation in the novel. The act of superimposition can be identified here, not only in terms of the different timescales of historical and evolutionary duration, but in terms of the coming together of time and space. The museological impulses exploited by Wells are articulations of both time and space, working through the imagining and realisation of one through the configuration of the other. Both take on the quality of medium within the Palace of Green Porcelain as an imaginative reiteration of the Crystal Palace. Overall, the sense of space in the novel is characterised by a peculiar sensation - it seems as that as the machine moves in time and not space, the Time Traveller never actually leaves his home. Subsequently, distinctions between interior and exterior are severely eroded.

The breadth of vision applied to the scope of museologically-orientated material culture, applicable to entire landscapes, is fused with the sense of artefactually rendered domestic intimacy found in the Time Traveller's home. The principle sites constructed in the narrative can be identified as three separate, yet overlaid zones. The first is that of the Time Traveller's home. The second is the general landscape of 802,701, and the third is the apocalyptic beach at the Earth's twilight. A fourth, interstitial, zone could also be added to this list in the form of the space of temporal transition experienced during time travel. These zones are overlaid in that they all occupy the same space at different times, although their geographical boundaries are not fixed. The space of 802,701 is mapped at a much larger scale than that of the 1890s, which can be generally limited to the Time Traveller's home, yet these spaces are inextricably linked. The details, connections and differences of these various zones accumulate to hint at a particular narrative relating to interior and exterior, reinforcing a peculiar sense that the Time Traveller is still contained within his domestic workshop as he journeys to the future and back again.

The Time Traveller's home is the zone that serves to both construct and anchor all others within the novel is a meticulously crafted environment in which the politicised tension that Wells depicts in the future is staged with equal, albeit codified, bluntness. This is a space symbolically rendered in a manner that contradicts the initial appearance of things. Suvin has drawn attention to the contrast of spatial register in the novel, which he argues is a common structural element in the scientific romances, characterised by a destructive newness encroaching upon the tranquillity of the Victorian environment. The inner and outer framework of the narrative is also seen by Suvin as a means of establishing this collision: 'The framework is set in surroundings as staid and familiarly Dickensian as possible, such as the cozy study of *The Time Machine*' (Suvin 1979, p.208). Yet what appears to be an environment of domestic refinement and comfort contains an explicit reference to the chairs upon which the guests in the Time Traveller's home sit: 'Our chairs, being his patents, embraced and caressed us rather than submitted to be sat upon' (Wells 1895, p.1).

Leon Stover, in his rigorous literary analysis of the novel, identifies the chairs as a direct reference to William Morris, designer, craftsman, writer and poet. As a leading figure in the Arts and Crafts Movement, Morris responded to Ruskin's call to arms:

In the coming decades, William Morris was to wage war on the factory-made ugliness of Victorian domestic interiors, and to expand, even more trenchantly than Ruskin himself, on the intimate connections between morality, as socially and privately understood, and design. (Wilson 2003, p.164)

That these chairs are uncannily comfortable sets up the Time Traveller in competition with Morris, who was the first to patent a cushioned chair with a backrest that could be inclined. This inexplicable quality suggests that Morris's patent has been surpassed. Although not named in the text, Morris is also one of the guests of the Time Traveller on the night of his return from the future. He is described, in a manner that is designed to be insulting, as 'a quiet, shy man with a beard – whom I didn't know, and who, as far as my observation went, never opened his mouth all the evening' (Wells 1895, p.19). The sophistication of the chair design in relation to anything that Morris had been able to build indicates an assumed superiority of social theory articulated within the narrative. *The Time Machine* is referentially set up as a favourable and surpassing comparison with Morris's own socialist utopian fantasy, *News from Nowhere* (1891). However, this rigidly deterministic reading ignores the very qualities that are supposed to indicate the politicisation of the chairs: their technological sophistication, the illusion of some form of agency as a result and the peculiar dissolution of a series of physical, psychic and technological boundaries. These chairs are prosthetic extensions that respond to a form of instrumental but unskilled control. The situation is described not in terms of a body in a chair, but as an erosion of distinctions between the two. The chairs are useful in sustaining a general sense of erosion throughout the narrative, which is mirrored in a general absence of distinction between interior and exterior in the future landscape, as well as by the negation of spatial distance implicit in the operation of time travel.

The relaxed atmosphere of the Time Traveller's domestic space contains other references that defy immediate impressions:

> The fire burnt brightly, and the soft radiance of the incandescent lights in the lilies of silver caught the bubbles that flashed and passed in out glasses. (...) , and there was that luxurious after-dinner atmosphere, when thought runs gracefully free of the trammels of precision. (Wells 1895, p.1)

Stover has identified the presence of two specific charges being made in this brief passage. The first of these addresses the condition of the lighting. The incandescence, made clear by later references to non-electric lighting, is generated by gas mantles. This is a jab at the failure of the entire district of Richmond, the location of the Time Traveller's house, to be electrified. In the convincing narrative Stover has constructed, which he argues would have been clearly identified by an audience in the 1890s; Wells is identifying a ruling class that has failed to take adequate control of the transformative processes of technological modernity (Stover 1996, pp.23-24).

The projected landscape and architecture of 802,701 clearly resembles that of the Crystal Palace at Sydenham. This is not just in reference to the connections drawn out already between the Palace of Green Porcelain, and the rebuilt Crystal Palace itself, but rather a suggested overlaying of the entire spatial zone of 802,701 onto the larger site of the building's extensive grounds. Other than the dinosaurs, a pair of Sphinxes either side of a staircase along one edge of the terraces that once formed the space in front of the building are among the few remains present among the ruins of the present-day Crystal Palace. As well as evoking the already declining grandeur of the Crystal Palace, and its narratives of progress, leisure, education and distraction, the landscape and architecture of 802,701 refers to a visual tradition that encompasses visual art and notions of ownership and power as traditionally English forms of authoritative meaning. They also, like the chairs in the Time Traveller's home, evoke alternative models of socially minded speculative fiction:

> The palaces and gardens suggest the landscape of neoclassical paintings and country houses, while alluding to a line of English utopian romances which would have been fresh in the minds of Wells's first readers: Richard Jefferies' *After London* (1885), W.H. Hudson's *A Crystal Age* (1887), and, above all, William Morris's *News from Nowhere* (1890). Morris's death in 1896 drew an affectionate if patronising acknowledgement in the Saturday Review – 'His dreamland was no futurity, but an illuminated past', Wells wrote. (Parrinder 1995, pp.42-43)

Again, like the chairs in the Time Traveller's home, there can be found a specific reference to Morris in *The Time Machine*. 802,701 at first seems like a future utopia, yet is proved to be an argument for its impossibility. Both this all encompassing landscape, and individual pieces of domestic furniture, alludes to the same point of reference. This accumulation upon a single point further erases any sense of clearly demarcated boundary between the various spaces and eras of *The Time Machine*. Instead, there is a suggested equivalence of materiality, and a sense of which both landscape and artefact are accessibly conceptualised as forms of material culture.

The site of the house itself is identified as in Richmond, south-west of Central London. However, this local geography is expanded by the Time Traveller's explorations of the landscape in the year 802,701. After the time machine is removed from its point of arrival, and dragged inside the base of the Sphinx, the Time Traveller is resolved to the idea of gathering knowledge about the future world, that might, in indirect form, lead back towards a solution of how to recover the machine. However, despite the increasing radius of his wandering survey, he still feels restricted to a space around his own home, and in an oblique manner limited by its virtual and enclosing presence: 'Yet a certain feeling, you may understand, tethered me in a circle of a few miles round the point of my arrival' (Wells 1895, p.66). This circle is in a sense both defined by and an extension of the Time Traveller's home as the focal site of the novel's spatial orientation. When seeking to recover his stolen machine, the quest of the Time Traveller could be imagined as a process of seeking to restore the altered landscape in which he finds himself to its original condition. Finding himself stuck in the future is to be cast away upon a distorted perversion of a familiar terrain. This perversion is taken to its most extreme form after the Time Traveller's escape from the year 802,701:

> The machine was standing on a sloping beach. The sea stretched away to the south-west, to rise into a sharp bright horizon against the wan sky. There were no breakers and no waves, for not a breath of wind was stirring. Only a slight oily swell rose and fell like a gentle breathing, and showed that the eternal sea was still moving and living. And along the margin where the water sometimes broke was a thick incrustation of salt – pink under the lurid sky. There was a sense of oppression in my head, and I noticed that I was breathing very fast. The sensations reminded me of my only experience of mountaineering, and from that I judged the air to be more rarefied than it is now. (Wells 1895, pp.136-137)

Rather than explore this monstrous scene by foot, by bodily moving about the beach, he explores by skipping forwards in time to observe changes and gain a better understanding of the circumstances around him. He travels in strides across time, rather than through a vulnerable clamber across the beach.

Yet spatially, his existence is still narrowly defined, and metaphorically contained within that of not only his own time, but I would suggest his own space. His only connection to the sanity and substance of his time is to be physically in contact with the machine, to be touching it or seated upon it at all times. In response to a thickening darkness of the sky, the Time Traveller becomes nauseous with horror, his body shivering and breathing becoming painful. To be detached from the machine in this extreme perversion of his own familiar spatial existence suggests nothing less than the annihilation of self, lying helpless within a world where humanity has long since ceased to exist, except perhaps in the strange form floating by the water's edge. This vision of portentous horror that the Time Traveller beholds on the sea shore forms one end of an arc that describes a space within the novel that is both consistent and yet multifarious. It is one that might be rendered as singular, yet comprised of glaring incompatibilities that jar and compete. The interior space of the house and workshop in Richmond both contains and is surrounded by the oily swell and desolate beach of the far future.

In *The Order of Things* by Michel Foucault, it is the arrangement of knowledge that creates man, or humanity, as a subject of knowledge (1997). That arrangement of knowledge suffers a profound collapse in *The Time Machine*. Foucault's notion of man as a recent invention is one that is both dramatically thematised in the novel, through the invention and subsequent death of man, and also serves as a methodological understanding of the novel. Man, for Foucault, is a being that constitutes the representations which themselves constitute the means of life. This representation is constituted from within the social existence of a human being, and frames and facilitates that existence. The constitution of an object of knowledge in this way becomes the means to represent itself. This qualitative sensation is one that I would like to overlay as a lens upon the material world of *The Time Machine*, as an object of knowledge that in part constitutes its own means of representation and understanding.

The prevalence of uncertainty as a destructive and threatening force is not limited to the embodied form of 'man', or rather the human subject as understood by the Time Traveller as that of his own present. The effect is one that is in part defined by the term abhuman. However, whereas Kelly Hurley's use of the abhuman refers to the ruination of the human subject as it is figured in the pages of gothic fiction in Britain in the late nineteenth century, its tendencies reach far beyond anatomically defined bodies in the novel, and pollute its entire fabric. The spectacle of not only bodies, but materiality, is offered through displays of matter, things, people, space and even temporality as metamorphic, undifferentiated, fragmented, and permeable. Uncertainty, together with the manifest tendencies of degeneration, as represented by the effects and appearances of abhuman bodies, dominates the presence of materiality and material culture in *The Time Machine*. The nature of that materiality and material culture is inescapably determined as text; as such all aspects of this material world are vulnerable to contamination by the abhuman - a literary manifestation of social anxiety.

There is a perhaps an echo of that embodiment of degenerative, self obsessed, narcissistic decadence with Des Esseintes, the protagonist of J.K. Huysmans *Á Rebours* (1884). Huysmans' proto-Eloi embarks on a trip from Paris to London, but before leaving the city decides that between his journey thus far, sensory experience and his own solipsistically involved reflections, he is able to constitute the trip and his stay in the foreign capital as in an internal, psychic experience. He returns home to enjoy his trip to London. The Time Traveller realises that in recognizing the social conflict of his own time in the future, he too has not left home (Stover 1996, p.2). Social metaphor not only serves to reinforce the idea of the space of the

Time Machine as a multifarious but singular conflation, but indeed relies on this very principle in order to function as dramatically within the novel as it does. Space, in this unique configuration, becomes a part of the binding substance of materiality and material culture. This constitutive presence within the novel is one that facilitates both diegetic momentum, and social metaphor.

The Palace of Green Porcelain is an embodiment of a distinct form of modernity as a museological form. It is a form constituted with some very specifically constructed elements. The Time Traveller's citing of South Kensington is an unambiguous reference to what is now known as the Victoria and Albert Museum in London. The Palace of Green Porcelain offers a specific site for an intersection of material culture and textual narrative in the images South Kensington and Sydenham. As a material world, the location of *The Time Machine* can be identified between the diegetic illusion of an adventure story, and the actualities Albertopolis and the Crystal Palace park. The ever-expanding arc that reaches between 1851 into futurity and the year 802,701 is characterised by the exhibitionary complex, Tony Bennett's description of an arrangement of institutional forms that are museological, but also encompass modes of public spectacle, and sites of commodity arrangement and exchange (1996). The exhibitionary complex orders objects on display while ordering the inspecting public, influencing the development of museological institutions and commodity circulation.

Bennett's exhibitionary complex is suggestive of spaces in which material culture is ordered and interpreted. Yet in *The Time Machine*, the presence of South Kensington as an originary site for such an exhibitionary complex is exploded to describe an entire material world. This world covers a temporal scheme of millions of years and encompasses landscape, climate, buildings and people. The world of *The Time Machine* is made in the image of South Kensington, but extended to the point at which materiality and material culture appear as something to which there is no exterior to.

But this is a nightmare vision of Albertopolis as an endless sprawl, in which order and stability are eradicated in favour of degeneration and uncertainty. In *The Time Machine*, material culture exceeds its containment by institutional forms, suggesting that such orderly containment might itself be nothing but a fantasy. This logic of the novel's constitution as a material world intersects with our present and past along the temporal trajectory from the Time Traveller's own version of South Kensington, historically binding this moment of futurity to the same hallucinatory dream.

And it is to a dream that Wells likens his own scientific romances, or rather, the experience of reading them is like a dream from which we awaken upon their completion. But this would be a dream of troubled reflection rather than the mythic and dream-worlds of spectacular modernity. Or alternatively, a dream of imagining things as other than they are. Unlike William Morris's *News From Nowhere* however, the dream as the literal thing itself doesn't generally function as a device in Wells'romances. Whereas Morris has William Guest simply fall asleep and 'awaken' within a dream in which he has somehow appeared in the future, the form of journey, its very possibility, is a part of the constitution of the material world of *The Time Machine*. It is the imagining of time as fourth dimension, as medium that can be traversed that makes this tale possible. Although Wells likens his scientific romances to dreaming, it is that this is a state from which one will awaken that is more significant. It is an analogy that depends on an ontological certainty that the dream and fantasy are not essentially other to wakefulness and reality. However, despite Wells' own distaste for using the dream as device, the dream as effect lingers and resonates as utopian form. And that it does so helps to reveal that it is the presence of utopia as impulse, or process, rather than as project, that is ultimately articulated by Wells both here and within his more explicitly utopian thinking.

Wells refers briefly to Morris within the text of *The Time Machine* instigating a direct and adversarial relationship with *News From Nowhere*, published five years previously. In Morris' utopia, a socialist with a hatred of modernity awakens in, or rather dreams of, a medieval fantasy of the future in which capitalism and technology have been left behind by a society favouring an egalitarian and rural existence. Morris's utopian dream is dismissed; to imagine progress in the image of a pre-capitalist, pre-industrial arcadia suggested no answer for Wells. And although his future is a nightmare, the momentum is still forward-looking in its call to action. But Wells was also unlike Morris in how he constructed his utopias. Morris took the process literally, and saw himself as a purveyor of pure authorial intent. There was no subtlety in his fantastic worlds. They were meant to represent in a clear, unclouded manner, the views of the author. Wells, on the other hand, constructs a narrative that is polemical, but utilises materiality as a set of raw materials for cognitive engagement, as well as estrangement. Rather than spell out a utopian fantasy, as a panorama of the present through a dream of what might be, *The Time Machine* explores aspects of utopian possibility. Wells' future, although addressed as a stark warning, is still a future, and therefore perhaps more utopian a discourse than Morris's nostalgic paradise. It is concerned with addressing, ultimately to facilitate resolution, the complexities and difficulties of the present moment, of not wallowing in fantasies of the past.

The space of the novel as a meditation on, or facilitation of, utopian thought and practice is articulated through a highly specific discursive engagement with material culture: material culture and dream are conflated within *The Time Machine*, as are science and philosophy, to construct a speculative form of utopian thought. In order to conclude we make a temporal shift here to a later work by Wells, *A Modern Utopia* (1905). In a very-self conscious epilogue to the book Wells as near as apologises for the presence of invented protagonists in the text, and in particular, for their centrality and antagonisms as the device through which the reader encounters this space of social alterity. Wells' preface to *A Modern Utopia*, from 1925 describes the book as an experiment in form that overlapped with the completion of his novel *Kipps*. He aimed for what he calls a sort of lucid vagueness. He rejects in this case the argumentative essay, clear divisions, binary oppositions, the hard, heavy black and white lines of yes and no. Neither did he wish to reduce this to 'stark' narrative. It is the outcome of trial and deliberation, intended to be as it is. He says: 'I am aiming throughout at a sort of shot-silk texture between philosophical discussion on the one hand and imaginative narrative on the other' (Wells 2005, p.6).

I'd like to suggest that this is a resonant metaphor to close with: The image of shot-silk, a warp and weft of differing colours, allowing for a contrasting and unstable oscillation of effect, changing when in movement or if seen from different points of view. We end up with a form of enquiry in which fiction is able to accommodate both science and philosophy as generators of doubt. After all, the perpetual sustaining of questions is, surely, the most honest and valuable form of enquiry.

The Palace of Green Porcelain is made in the image of South Kensington and the Crystal Palace. These originary sites of the exhibitionary complex are not only reconfigured as a building, but exploded to describe an entire material world. The world of *The Time Machine* is made in the image of South Kensington and the Crystal Palace, its evolutionary perversions reflected in the original intentionality of the Pitt Rivers collection. However, the novel's world is extended to the point at which materiality and material culture appear as something that it is impossible to stand outside of, as a museum from which you cannot exit. This interpretation of this novel as material culture is not aimed at considering *The Time Machine* as an artefact, as printed book, but rather as a rich, complex material world, forged by the forces of modernity unleashed by the Great Exhibition, occupying a literary and psychic space somewhere between actuality and illusion.

References

Joseph Addison, from *The Spectator*, no 26, 30th March 1711, cited in Martin Myrone and Christopher Frayling (Eds) *The Gothic Reader: A Critical Anthology*, Tate, London 2006.

Marc Augé, *Non-Places: Introduction to an Anthropology of Supermodernity*, Verso, London and New York 1995.

Jean Baudrillard, Symbolic Exchange and Death, Sage London 1993.

Jean Baudrillard, The Spirit of Terrorism, Verso, London and New York, 2002.

Stephen Bayley, *The Albert Memorial: The Monument in its Social and Architectural Context*, Scolar Press, London 1981.

Patrick Beaver, *The Crystal Palace*, Phillimore, Chichester 1993. P.84.

C.A. Bell-Knight, *The Crystal Palace: The Rise and Fall of the Biggest Ever Glass Container*, C.A. Bell-Knight, London 1976.

Walter Benjamin, *The Arcades Project*, Belknap Press, Cambridge and London 1999.

Walter Benjamin, 'The Sock' from 'Final Version' (1938) of *Berlin Childhood Around 1900*, Belknap Press, Cambridge and London 2006.

Tony Bennet, 'The Exhibitionary Complex', in Greenberg, Ferguson and Nairne (Eds.), *Thinking About Exhibitions*, Routledge, London and New York 1996.

Beatrice Blackwood, 'The Classification of Artefacts in the Pitt Rivers Museum, Oxford.' *Occasional Papers on Technology* No.11. Pitt Rivers Museum, University of Oxford 1970.

Beatrice Blackwood, *The Origin and Development of the Pitt Rivers Museum*, Pitt Rivers Museum, Oxford 1991.

Ernst Bloch, The Principle of Hope, MIT Press, Cambridge 1995.

Mark Bowden, *Pitt Rivers: The life and archaeological work of Lieutenant-General Augustus Henry Lane Fox Pitt Rivers, DCL,*

FRS, FSA, Cambridge University Press, Cambridge 1991.

Chris Brooks, *Gothic Revival,* Phaidon, London 1999.

Susan Buck-Morss, *The Dialectics of Seeing: Walter Benjamin and the Arcades Project,* Cambridge and London, MIT Press 1993.

Judith Butler, *Bodies That Matter: On the Discursive Limits of 'Sex',* Routeldge, New York and London 1993.

Deborah Cadbury, *The Dinosaur Hunters: A True Story of Scientific Rivalry andthe Discovery of the Prehistoric World,* Fourth Estate, London 2000.

Jacques Derrida, *Of Grammatology,* John Hopkins University Press, Baltimore 1997.

Mark Dion in conversation with Miwon Kwon in Kwon (Ed.) *Mark Dion,* Phaidon, London 1997.

Jack Flam, (Ed.) *Robert Smithson: The Collected Writings,* University of California Press, Berkeley 1996.

Henri Focillon, *The Life of Forms of Art, Zone Books,* Cambridge 1992.

Michel Foucault, *The Order of Things: An Archaeology of the Human Sciences,* Routledge, London 1997.

Stephen Jay Gould, *Ever since Darwin,* Pelican, Harmondsworth 1987.

Stephen Jay Gould, 'The Power of Narrative', in *An Urchin in the Storm: Essays About Books and Ideas,* Penguin, London, 1990.

Paul Greenhalgh, *Ephemeral Vistas: The Expositions Universelles, Great Exhibitions and World Fairs,1851-1939,* Manchester University Press, Manchester 1988.

Hildi Hawkins and Danielle Olsen (Eds.), *The Phantom Museum,* Profile Books, London 2003.

Kelly Hurley *The Gothic Body: Sexuality, Materialism and Degeneration at the Fin de Siècle,* Cambridge University Press, Cambridge 1996.

Kelly Hurley, *The Gothic Body, Sexuality, Materialism, and Degeneration at the Fin De Siecle,* Cambridge University Press, Cambridge 1996.

George Gilbert Scott in *Handbook to the Prince Consort National Memorial, Published by authority of the Executive Committee*, John Murray, London 1874.

Edward James, 'Science Fiction by Gaslight: An Introduction to English-Language Science Fiction in the Nineteenth Century', in David Seed (Ed.) *Anticipations: Essays on Early Science Fiction and its Precursors*, , Liverpool University Press, Liverpool 1995.

Steve McCarthy and Mick Gilbert, *The Crystal Palace Dinosaurs: The Story of the World's First Prehistoric Sculptures*, The Crystal Palace Foundation, London 1994.

Tom Moylan, *Scraps of Untainted Sky: Science Fiction, Utopia, Dystopia*, Westview Press, Boulder 2000.

J.L. Myers (Ed), *Lt.Gen A. Lane Fox Pitt Rivers: The Evolution of Culture and Other Essays*, Clarendon Press, Oxford 1906.

Max Nordau, *Degeneration*, University of Nebraska Press, Lincoln and London 1993.

Bjornar Olsen, 'Roland Barthes: From Sign to Text' in Christopher Tilley (Ed.), *Reading Material Culture: Structuralism, Hermeneutics and Post Structuralism*, Basil Blackwell, Oxford and Cambridge Mass 1990.

Patrick Parrinder (Ed.), *H. G. Wells: The Critical Heritage*, Routledge and Kegan Paul, London and Boston 1972.

Patrick Parrinder, *Shadows of the Future: H.G. Wells, Science Fiction and Prophecy*, Liverpool University Press, Liverpool 1995.

Patrick Parrinder, 'Introduction' in H.G. Wells, *A Modern Utopia*, Penguin London 2005.Susan M. Pearce, 'Introduction' in Pearce (Ed.) *Interpreting Objects and Collections*, Routledge, London and New York 1996.

Samuel Phillips, *Guide to the Crystal Palace and Park*, Crystal Palace Library and Bradbury and Evans, London 1856.

Donald Preziosi and Louise A. Hitchcock, *Aegean Art and Architecture*, Oxford University Press, Oxford 1999.

Brian Stableford, 'Frankenstein and the Origins of Science Fiction', in David Seed (Ed.) *Anticipations: Essays on Early Science Fiction and its Precursors*, , Liverpool University Press, Liverpool 1995.

Gavin Stamp, 'George Gilbert Scott, the Memorial Competition, and the Critics,' in Chris Brooks (Ed.) *The Albert Memorial: The Prince Consort National Memorial: Its History, Contexts and Conservation*, Yale University Press, New Haven and London 2000.

Leon Stover (Ed.), *H.G. Wells, The Time Machine: An Invention: A Critical Text of the The Time MachineLondon First Edition, with an Introduction and Appendices*, McFarland and Company, Jefferson and London 1996.

Boris and Arkady Strugatsky, *Roadside Picnic*, Gollancz, London 2007.

Darko Suvin, *Metamorphoses of Science Fiction: On the Poetics and History of a Literary Genre*, Yale University Press, New Haven and London 1979.

Christopher Tilley, *Material Culture and Text: The Art of Ambiguity*, Routledge, London and New York 1991.

Graeme Tytler, *Physiognomy in the European Novel: Faces and Fortunes*, Princeton University Press, New Jersey 1982. H.G. Wells, *The Time Machine: An Invention*, Heinemann, London 1895.

Ratan Vaswani, *Museums Journal*, January 2001.

H.G. Wells, Authorial Preface to *The Scientific Romances of H.G. Wells*, Gollancz, London 1933.

H.G. Wells, *The Time Machine: An Invention*, Heinemann, London 1895.

H.G. Wells, Authorial Preface to *A Modern Utopia*, Penguin, London 2005.

A.N. Wilson, *The Victorians*, Arrow Books, London 2003.

Contemporary culture has eliminated both the concept of the public and the figure of the intellectual. Former public spaces – both physical and cultural – are now either derelict or colonized by advertising. A cretinous anti-intellectualism presides, cheerled by expensively educated hacks in the pay of multinational corporations who reassure their bored readers that there is no need to rouse themselves from their interpassive stupor. The informal censorship internalized and propagated by the cultural workers of late capitalism generates a banal conformity that the propaganda chiefs of Stalinism could only ever have dreamt of imposing. Zer0 Books knows that another kind of discourse – intellectual without being academic, popular without being populist – is not only possible: it is already flourishing, in the regions beyond the striplit malls of so-called mass media and the neurotically bureaucratic halls of the academy. Zer0 is committed to the idea of publishing as a making public of the intellectual. It is convinced that in the unthinking, blandly consensual culture in which we live, critical and engaged theoretical reflection is more important than ever before.